Four Pillars of Destiny
Practical Ten Gods

Dr. Jin Peh
Edited by
Miranda van Gaalen,
Carolyn McCallum, Julio Richero
and Crystal Al-Shatti

Copyright 2022
Dr. Peh Chong Jin

All rights reserved. No part of this publication may be reproduced or utilized in any form or by any means, electronic or mechanical, including printing, photocopying, uploading to the web, recording, or by any information storage and retrieval system, or used in another book, without specific written permission from the author, except for short fully credited extracts or quotes used for review purposes.

Disclaimer:

The information presented in this book should not be considered a substitute for a professional Chinese astrology reading.

ISBN: 978-1-7329155-1-0
Kindle Direct Publishing

Foreword

When I first started studying with Lily Chung in San Francisco back in 2009, she told me that the Ten Gods method had inspired her to start studying Bazi seriously. Her younger brother had bought a Chinese book about the Ten Gods method of Bazi and started analyzing Bazi charts as a result. It was written that if a woman has a mix of Power elements (i.e. of both polarities) in her chart, then she had loose morals. Her brother looked at Lily's chart, noticed the mix of Power elements and said that she was a questionable woman. While she was extremely upset with this statement, Lily was also extremely motivated to start studying Bazi to prove her brother and the statement wrong. And that is how her journey started in 1986.

With this in mind, I have not included teachings related to his method in classes over the years as the traditional Ten Gods books listed a wide range of statements that could not be substantiated. In addition, some of the statements could not be applied to modern living or could be considered offensive, like the one that Lily's brother made to her. However, with the pandemic, Lily had more time and so she started exploring the Ten Gods method in detail. She was then able to start teaching her findings and conclusions remotely.

In 2021, travel was still very much affected by the pandemic and as a result, I could only study with Lily through Zoom rather than in person in San Francisco. She was extremely generous in sharing with me her thoughts about the Ten Gods. As with everything else that I have learnt over the years, there was a period of digestion and reflection before I was able to internalize this information and incorporate it into my readings and teachings. I spent time finding celebrity examples that were able to confirm and substantiate the theories that

Lily taught me. Findings that were vague or did not stand up to further analysis were left out, as well as those that were too complex for readers who are not that familiar with Bazi.

The focus of this book is not on simplifying the Ten Gods method. Rather, it is to show readers a more coherent, structured and responsible approach in which each finding can be accounted for by many real life examples. It is more practical and less theoretical and also takes into account how life has progressed since the old Chinese texts were written.

The Ten Gods method refers to the five aspects of a person's life as seen through Bazi. In Chinese, it is called the Shi Shen, so it can be translated as the Ten Gods, Spirits or Essences. It essentially refers to the Output (Creativity or Expression), Power (Authority), Resource (Parents or Family Background), Wealth (Salary or Investments) and Rivals (Siblings or Competitors) in life. The seven chapters then discuss the theories in detail with many practical examples. As there are more theories associated with Output and Power, they are assigned two chapters each, while there is only one chapter for Wealth, Resource and Rivals.

Unlike other books where the reader has to flip to the appendix or to the introduction, I decided to include the relevant reference tables within the chapters themselves so that the reader is able to follow the steps in deriving the theories. This is why I have repeated the 12 Life Stage Cycles several times in the different chapters. It is my way of ensuring that the reader is able to follow.

Another new approach that I have adopted for this book is to bold the Day Stems and the relevant Pillars that are discussed within the chart. This allows the reader to make the association between the Day Stems and the relevant aspect that is being discussed, be it Wealth, Resource or Output. Note that this is not the usual way of presenting a Bazi chart.

As for the examples, I have made a special effort to include the Special Pillars that can be found in the hour. They have been highlighted in the tables.

Here is the chronology of how this book was written:

First up, my teacher Lily Chung taught me her Ten Gods theories remotely from San Francisco to Dubai in the summer of 2021. I am grateful for her generosity in sharing her findings and faith in me to propagate them to my students and readers.

After a year of finding my own examples and substantiating the theories, I have to thank my trustworthy team of editors from around the world.

Miranda van Gaalen, thank you for combing through what I have written in detail and for pointing out anything that is incongruent or does not stand up. I am glad that we are able to meet in Arnhem in the Netherlands again after a few years of restricted travel.

Carolyn McCallum, thank you always for your support and for your questions. That is the best way to study any subject and I thank you for your detailed eye. I look forward to seeing you soon in Australia, either in your hometown of Sydney or in Noosa.

Julio Richero, thank you for clarifying the birthdays and charts of all the examples that I have used. Thank you to you and your mother Griselda for your support over in Buenos Aires and Los Angeles respectively.

Crystal Al Shatti, thank you for being my Middle Eastern patroness and for your positive energy and laughter. Thank you for formulating and preparing my course books and for your support.

The script was then sent to my designer Josephine Wong over in Hong Kong, who then found the cover and prepared this book for publishing.

I also would like to thank my organizers from around the world who have helped me connect with my students.

Irina Anfinogenova, thank you always for your support for the classes in Moscow that are now being done remotely. Thank you for organizing the Russian version of the 60 Personalities book and I look forward to more Russian translations of my books in the future.

Zulima Kushu, thank you always for your good advice and enthusiasm in answering my questions.

Janene and Bruce Laird, thank you to my Aussie parents for your love and support always. The pandemic has made us family for life. I look forward to visiting you in Noosa.

Petra Coll Exposito, thank you for organizing my classes in Germany and Europe. Thank you for your faith and support to bringing me to a new audience. I would also like to thank my German translator Caroline Wolff for her enthusiasm, emotional strength and support.

Andrea Szomuru, thank you for your bubbly energy and for being one of my biggest fans. Your smiles and positive thoughts are always appreciated.

Luca Pisano and Alison Yeung, thank you always for your friendship and support. It was my pleasure to edit and write this book in your lovely home in Turin during the summer of 2022. We have come a long way since those Taipei days more than 20 years ago.

And thank you to my siblings Sylvia, Linda and Ghee for their belief in and support of my work.

For my mother, it was great to see you in Singapore in April 2022 when Singapore opened to the rest of the world and thank you for making me who I am today.

And for my father, thank you for watching over me always. I hope this makes you proud.

You can also follow me on Twitter @drjinpeh.

Dedicated to my father Peh Kong Wan
(July 22, 1941 to April 24, 2021)

Contents

Foreword		iii
List of Tables and Examples		2
Chapter One	Introduction	18
Chapter Two	Direct Power	28
Chapter Three	Seven Killings	62
Chapter Four	Eating God	102
Chapter Five	Hurting Officer	136
Chapter Six	Wealth	164
Chapter Seven	Resource	186
Chapter Eight	Rivals	216
Chapter Nine	Conclusion	236

List of Tables and Examples

Chapter One Introduction

Table 1.1	Day Stem with Direct Power and Seven Killings
Table 1.2	Day Stem with Eating God and Hurting Officer
Table 1.3	Day Stem with Direct Wealth and Indirect Wealth
Table 1.4	Day Stem with Direct Resource and Indirect Resource
Table 1.5	Day Stem with Sibling and Rob Wealth
Table 1.6	12 Branches with hidden Stems
Table 1.7	12 Branches and hidden Stems with classification
Table 1.8	Element and Three Harmony Combination
Table 1.9	Element and Seasonal Combination

Chapter Two Direct Power

Table 2.1	Day Stem and Direct Power
Table 2.2	Day Stems and Nobleman Stars
Table 2.3	Day Stem and Direct Power Sitting on the Nobleman Pillars
Table 2.4	Month Branches with Solar and Lunar Helpers
Table 2.5	Day Stem and Direct Power as Solar or Lunar Helper
Table 2.6	Stem with Academic Star and Direct Power Stem
Table 2.7	Day Stem and Direct Power on the Academic Star Pillars
Table 2.8	12 Life Stages for the Direct Power Yang Stems
Table 2.9	12 Life Stages for the Direct Power Yin Stems

Table 2.10	Day Stem with Direct Power on the Prosperity Pillar
Table 2.11	Day Stem, Direct Power and the Branch with hidden Wealth and Direct Power Stem
Table 2.12	Six Days Sitting on a Branch with Wealth producing Direct Power

Example	Name	Profession
2.1	Susan Boyle	Scottish Singer
2.2	Jessica Simpson	American Singer and Actress
2.3	Billie Eilish	American Singer-Songwriter
2.4	Coco Chanel	French Fashion Designer
2.5	Lindsey Buckingham	American Musician and Singer
2.6	Donald Glover	American Actor and Musician
2.7	Harry Styles	English Singer-Songwriter and Actor
2.8	Kristi Yamaguchi	American Figure Skater
2.9	Queen Elizabeth the Queen Mother	British Royalty
2.10	Carlos Santana	Mexican-American Guitarist
2.11	Ivana Trump	American Businesswoman and Model
2.12	Gordon Ramsay	British Chef and Restaurateur
2.13	Sir Ian McKellen	English Actor
2.14	Dana Carvey	American Actor and Comedian
2.15	Gene Simmons	Israeli-American Singer-Songwriter and Musician
2.16	Dilma Rousseff	President of Brazil 2011 to 2016
2.17	Harper Lee	American Novelist
2.18	Rickie Lee Jones	American Singer
2.19	John McEnroe	American Tennis Player

2.20	Jean Dujardin	French Actor
2.21	Matt Damon	American Actor
2.22	Paul Simon	American Singer and Musician
2.23	Courteney Cox	American Actress
2.24	Jessica Chastain	American Actress
2.25	Arnold Schwarzenegger	Austrian-American Actor and Politician
2.26	Bradley Cooper	American Actor and Filmmaker
2.27	Julio Iglesias	Spanish Singer-Songwriter
2.28	Michelle Williams	American Actress
2.29	Lucy Liu	American Actress
2.30	Vanessa Paradis	French Singer and Actress
2.31	David Beckham	English Footballer
2.32	Herb Elliott	Australian Athlete
2.33	Robert Mitchum	American Actor
2.34	Pierre Cardin	Italian-French Designer
2.35	Gladys Knight	American Singer and Actress
2.36	Johnny Depp	American Actor and Musician
2.37	Martha Stewart	American Television Personality
2.38	Francis Ford Coppola	American Film Director
2.39	Rihanna	Barbadian Singer and Actress
2.40	Abdullah II of Jordan	Jordanian Royalty
2.41	Jon Bon Jovi	American Singer and Actor
2.42	Jane Fonda	American Actress
2.43	Jackie Chan	Hong Kong Actor and Martial Artist

Chapter Three Seven Killings

Table 3.1	Day Stem and Seven Killings
Table 3.2	Day Stem and Seven Killings Sitting on the Earth Branch in the Year Pillar
Table 3.3	Day Stem and Seven Killings Sitting on the Earth Branch in the Hour Pillar
Table 3.4	Day Stem and Hour Pillar with Seven Killings

Example	Name	Profession
3.1	Al Jarreau	American Singer and Musician
3.2	Taraji P. Henson	American Actress
3.3	Gary Cooper	American Actor
3.4	Anne Bancroft	American Actress
3.5	Steven Seagal	American Actor and Martial Artist
3.6	Ava Gardner	American Actress
3.7	Kate Moss	English Model and Businesswoman
3.8	Sam Shepard	American Actor and Playwright
3.9	Wendy Williams	American Television Host
3.10	Charley Pride	American Singer and Baseball Player
3.11	Jeanne Crain	American Actress
3.12	Zucchero	Italian Singer and Musician
3.13	Kirk Douglas	American Actor
3.14	Gianni Versace	Italian Fashion Designer
3.15	Sir Ridley Scott	English Filmmaker
3.16	Sir Laurence Olivier	English Actor and Director
3.17	Serge Gainsbourg	French Singer and Actor
3.18	Andrea Bocelli	Italian Singer-Songwriter

3.19	Richard Gere	American Actor
3.20	Shane Filan	Irish Singer
3.21	Steve Carell	American Actor and Comedian
3.22	Jordin Sparks	American Singer-Songwriter and Actress
3.23	Isabelle Adjani	French Actress
3.24	Morgan Freeman	American Actor
3.25	Andrew Garfield	British and American Actor
3.26	Kim Wilde	English Singer and Television Presenter
3.27	Mother Teresa	Albanian-Indian Nun and Missionary
3.28	Gaspard Ulliel	French Actor and Model
3.29	Harry Belafonte	Jamaican-American Singer and Actor
3.30	Jerry Lewis	American Actor and Comedian
3.31	Barbara Mandrell	American Country Singer
3.32	Sir Mick Jagger	English Singer and Actor
3.33	Kenny Rogers	American Singer and Actor
3.34	Betty White	American Actress and Comedian
3.35	Dame Joanna Lumley	English Actress and Comedian
3.36	Gerard Depardieu	French Actor
3.37	Baron Andrew Lloyd Webber	English Composer and Musical Theatre Impresario
3.38	Mae West	American Actress and Singer
3.39	Garry Kasparov	Russian Chess Grandmaster
3.40	Jeremy Irons	English Actor
3.41	Taylor Swift	American Singer-Songwriter
3.42	Diane Warren	American Songwriter
3.43	Philippe Starck	French Architect and Designer

3.44	Montserrat Caballe	Spanish Soprano
3.45	Audrey Hepburn	British Actress and Humanitarian
3.46	George Michael	English Singer-Songwriter
3.47	Bjork	Icelandic Singer and Actress
3.48	Luc Besson	French Film Director
3.49	Diana Ross	American Singer and Actress
3.50	David Gilmour	English Musician
3.51	Shaun White	American Snowboarder and Skateboarder
3.52	Chrissie Hynde	American Singer-Songwriter and Musician
3.53	Jean-Paul Gaultier	French Fashion Designer
3.54	Freddy Heineken	Dutch Businessman
3.55	Susan Sarandon	American Actress
3.56	Clint Eastwood	American Actor and Filmmaker
3.57	Sylvester Stallone	American Actor
3.58	Chuck Norris	American Actor and Martial Artist
3.59	Don Henley	American Singer and Musician
3.60	Sir Anthony Hopkins	Welsh Actor
3.61	Jane Birkin	English-French Actress and Singer
3.62	Robert Redford	American Actor and Director
3.63	Sir Elton John	English Singer-Songwriter and Pianist
3.64	Niki Lauda	Austrian Racing Car Driver
3.65	Catherine Deneuve	French Actress

Chapter Four Eating God

Table 4.1	Day Stem and Eating God
Table 4.2	Day Stem and Eating God Sitting on the Earth Branch
Table 4.3	Day Stem, Eating God, Combination Branch and the Hidden Stem within the Branch
Table 4.4	Day Stem and Eating God Combination Pillar
Table 4.5	12 Life Stages for the Eating God Yang Stems
Table 4.6	12 Life Stages for the Eating God Yin Stems
Table 4.7	Day Stem and Eating God Sitting on the Birth Branch Pillar

Example	Name	Profession
4.1	John Cameron Mitchell	American Actor and Playwright
4.2	Ilie Nastase	Romanian Tennis Player
4.3	Nicki Minaj	Trinidadian-American Rapper and Singer
4.4	John Wayne	American Actor
4.5	Keshia Knight Pulliam	American Actress
4.6	Thaksin Shinawatra	Thai Prime Minister 2001 to 2006
4.7	Cat Stevens	British Singer-Songwriter and Musician
4.8	Al Pacino	American Actor and Filmmaker
4.9	Saif Ali Khan	Indian Actor
4.10	Marlene Dietrich	German-American Actress and Singer
4.11	Ryan Gosling	Canadian Actor
4.12	Queen Elizabeth 2	British Royalty
4.13	Li Na	Chinese Tennis Player

4.14	Carles Puigdemont	Spanish Politician and Journalist
4.15	Sir Ringo Starr	English Singer-Songwriter and Musician
4.16	Oliver Stone	American Film Director
4.17	Chico Bouchiki	French Musician
4.18	Melanie Chisholm	English Singer-Songwriter
4.19	Donatella Versace	Italian Fashion Designer and Businesswoman
4.20	Sally Field	American Actress
4.21	Lenny Kravitz	American Singer and Actor
4.22	Marti Pellow	Scottish Singer
4.23	Jake Gyllenhaal	American Actor
4.24	Val Kilmer	American Actor
4.25	Stevie Wonder	American Singer and Musician
4.26	Ronald Isley	American Singer-Songwriter
4.27	Agnetha Faltskog	Swedish Singer and Actress
4.28	Tony Parker	French-American Basketball Player
4.29	Eminem	American Rapper
4.30	Chris Evans	American Actor
4.31	Kirsten Dunst	American Actress
4.32	Sir Cameron MacKintosh	British Theatrical Producer
4.33	Gustavo Kuerten	Brazilian Tennis Player
4.34	Karen Carpenter	American Singer and Drummer
4.35	Sir Sean Connery	Scottish Actor
4.36	Keith Carradine	American Actor and Singer
4.37	Conan O'Brien	American Television Host and Comedian
4.38	Jerry Lewis	American Actor and Comedian

4.39	Laura Dern	American Actress
4.40	Randy Couture	American Wrestler and Actor
4.41	Dakota Johnson	American Actress and Model
4.42	Robert Downey Jr.	American Actor
4.43	Freddie Prinze Jr.	American Actor
4.44	Loreena McKennit	Canadian Singer and Musician
4.45	Greg Kinnear	American Actor
4.46	Bonnie Raitt	American Singer and Guitarist
4.47	Ritchie Blackmore	English Singer and Guitarist

Chapter Five Hurting Officer

Table 5.1	Day Stem and Hurting Officer
Table 5.2	Day Stem and Hurting Officer Sitting on the Resource Pillars
Table 5.3	Days Sitting on the Hurting Officer

Example	Name	Profession
5.1	Dawn Fraser	Australian Swimmer
5.2	Goldie Hawn	American Actress
5.3	Jared Leto	American Actor and Singer
5.4	Jean-Paul Belmondo	French Actor
5.5	Jimmy Barnes	Australian Singer-Songwriter
5.6	Vincent Cassel	French Actor
5.7	Alain Prost	French Racing Driver
5.8	Nelson Mandela	South African President 1994 to 1999
5.9	Prince Andrew, Duke of York	British Royalty

5.10	Robert Stigwood	Australian-British Music Producer and Impresario
5.11	Tina Fey	American Actress and Comedian
5.12	Louis Tomlinson	English Singer
5.13	Bryce Dallas Howard	American Actress
5.14	Chris Pratt	American Actor
5.15	Drew Barrymore	American Actress and Filmmaker
5.16	Andre Agassi	American Tennis Player
5.17	Vivien Leigh	British Actress
5.18	Megan Fox	American Actress and Model
5.19	Renee Zellweger	American Actress
5.20	Jodie Foster	American Actress and Director
5.21	Venus Williams	American Tennis Player
5.22	Lily Tomlin	American Actress and Comedian
5.23	Doris Day	American Actress and Singer
5.24	Jimmy Page	English Musician and Singer
5.25	Lee Kuan Yew	Singaporean Prime Minister 1965 to 1990
5.26	Jose Feliciano	Puerto Rican Singer and Musician
5.27	Debbie Gibson	American Singer and Actress
5.28	Matthew McConaughey	American Actor
5.29	Stephanie Seymour	American Model and Actress
5.30	Sarah Brightman	English Singer and Actress
5.31	Halle Berry	American Actress
5.32	Kathleen Turner	American Actress
5.33	Jennifer Aniston	American Actress
5.34	Lucy Lawless	New Zealand Actress

5.35	Gloria Vanderbilt	American Heiress and Fashion Designer
5.36	Jennifer Lopez	American Actress and Singer
5.37	Christina Onassis	Greek Businesswoman
5.38	Raquel Welch	American Actress
5.39	Khloe Kardashian	American Media Personality
5.40	Kate Beckinsale	English Actress and Model

Chapter Six Wealth

Table 6.1	Day Stem with Direct Wealth and Indirect Wealth
Table 6.2	Yang Day Stem Combining with the Wealth element

Example	Name	Profession
6.1	Kristen Stewart	American Actress
6.2	Madonna	American Singer and Actress
6.3	Mae West	American Actress and Singer
6.4	Simon Le Bon	English Singer and Musician
6.5	Athina Onassis	French-Greek Heiress and Equestrian
6.6	George Clooney	American Actor and Filmmaker
6.7	Melanie Laurent	French Actress
6.8	Michael Jordan	American Basketball Player
6.9	Tom Cruise	American Actor
6.10	Vin Diesel	American Actor
6.11	Lisa Kudrow	American Actress
6.12	Gabriela Sabatini	Argentine Tennis Player
6.13	Steve Wozniak	American Electronics Engineer

6.14	Sultan Hassanal Bolkiah	Bruneian Royalty
6.15	Freddie Mercury	British Singer
6.16	Kylie Jenner	American Media Personality
6.17	Frankie Valli	American Singer
6.18	Gary Barlow	English Singer-Songwriter
6.19	Liz Hurley	English Actress and Model
6.20	Paris Hilton	American Media Personality
6.21	Pamela Anderson	Canadian-American Actress and Model
6.22	Jeremy Irons	English Actor
6.23	Tina Turner	American-Swiss Singer and Actress
6.24	Paul Theroux	American Writer and Novelist
6.25	Denzel Washington	American Actor and Director
6.26	Charlotte Casiraghi	Monegasque Royalty
6.27	Kesha	American Singer-Songwriter
6.28	Ashton Kutcher	American Actor and Entrepreneur
6.29	Adrien Brody	American Actor and Producer
6.30	Novak Djokovic	Serbian Tennis Player
6.31	Conan O'Brien	American Television Host and Comedian
6.32	Robert Redford	American Actor and Director
6.33	Benedict Cumberbatch	English Actor
6.34	Kaley Cuoco	American Actress
6.35	Sir Michael Palin	English Comedian, Actor and Television Presenter

Chapter Seven Resource

Table 7.1	Day Stem and Direct and Indirect Resource
Table 7.2	12 Life Stages for the Yang Resource Stems
Table 7.3	12 Life Stages for the Yin Resource Stems
Table 7.4	Resource Sitting on the Birth Pillar
Table 7.5	Day Stem and Seven Killings
Table 7.6	Day Stem with Resource Sitting on the Seven Killings Pillars

Example	Name	Profession
7.1	Mila Kunis	American Actress
7.2	Harvey Weinstein	American Film Producer
7.3	Anthony Perkins	American Actor and Director
7.4	Jessica Biel	American Actress and Model
7.5	Chaz Bono	American Writer
7.6	Seann William Scott	American Actor
7.7	Marion Cotillard	French Actress
7.8	Alexander Skarsgard	Swedish Actor
7.9	Arnold Schwarzenegger	Austrian-American Actor and Politician
7.10	Hilary Duff	American Actress and Singer
7.11	Bernie Madoff	American Financier
7.12	Gwen Stefani	American Singer-Songwriter and Actress
7.13	Cher	American Singer and Actress
7.14	Adam Levine	American Singer-Songwriter
7.15	Emma Stone	American Actress
7.16	David Chokachi	American Actor

7.17	Leonard Cohen	Canadian Singer and Poet
7.18	Adam Brody	American Actor
7.19	J.K. Rowling	British Author
7.20	Infanta Elena of Spain	Spanish Royalty
7.21	Diane Warren	American Songwriter
7.22	Will Young	British Singer and Actor
7.23	Anni-Frid Lyngstad	Norwegian-Swedish Singer
7.24	Hugh Hefner	American Magazine Publisher
7.25	Celine Dion	Canadian Singer
7.26	Jean-Claude Van Damme	Belgian Actor and Martial Artist
7.27	Geri Halliwell	English Singer
7.28	Anne Heche	American Actress
7.29	Jennifer Lopez	American Actress and Singer
7.30	James Franco	American Actor
7.31	Sylvester Stallone	American Actor
7.32	Lance Bass	American Singer and Actor
7.33	Dave Franco	American Actor
7.34	Anne, Princess Royal	British Royalty
7.35	Chuck Norris	American Actor and Martial Artist
7.36	Liam Payne	English Singer-Songwriter
7.37	Robert Redford	American Actor and Director
7.38	Meryl Streep	American Actress
7.39	Michael J. Fox	American Actor and Comedian
7.40	Shane Filan	Irish Singer

Chapter Eight Rivals

Table 8.1	Day Stem, Sibling and Rob Wealth
Table 8.2	12 Life Stages for the Yang Rival Stems
Table 8.3	12 Life Stages for the Yin Rival Stems
Table 8.4	Day Stem and Rivals Sitting on the Birth, Peak or Arrival

Example	Name	Profession
8.1	George Harrison	English Singer-Songwriter and Musician
8.2	Kate Winslet	English Actress
8.3	Mel Brown	English Singer and Television Personality
8.4	Robbie Williams	English Singer-Songwriter
8.5	Ron Howard	American Director and Actor
8.6	Frida Kahlo	Mexican Painter
8.7	Milo Ventimiglia	American Actor
8.8	Steven Spielberg	American Film Director
8.9	Lindsay Lohan	American Actress and Singer
8.10	Harrison Ford	American Actor
8.11	Serena Williams	American Tennis Player
8.12	Steve Winwood	English Singer and Musician
8.13	Dame Julie Walters	English Actress and Comedian
8.14	Heidi Klum	German-American Model
8.15	Lynn Anderson	American Country Singer
8.16	Fred Astaire	American Actor and Dancer
8.17	Drew Barrymore	American Actress and Filmmaker
8.18	Joyce Carol Oates	American Writer

8.19	Heather Graham	American Actress
8.20	Billy Joel	American Singer-Songwriter and Pianist
8.21	Jason Schwartzman	American Actor
8.22	Rami Malek	American Actor
8.23	Brody Jenner	American Television Personality
8.24	Naomi Watts	British Actress
8.25	Ellen Burstyn	American Actress
8.26	Gerard Butler	Scottish Actor
8.27	Miranda Lambert	American Country Singer
8.28	Amy Adams	American Actress
8.29	Billy Dee Williams	American Actor
8.30	Henry Cavill	British Actor

Chapter One

Chapter One Introduction

The Ten Gods refer to the ten different relationships of the Day Stem to the other Ten Stems. There are five different relationships to consider, which are derived from the Cycles of Production and Control of the five elements:

  i. The element that produces the Day Stem is Resource.
  ii. The element that the Day Stem produces is Output.
  iii. The element that the Day Stem controls is Wealth.
  iv. The element that controls the Day Stem is Power.
  v. The element that is the same as the Day Stem is the Rival.

As the Stems can either by Yang or Yin, there are two different types of Resource, Output, Wealth, Power and Rival, which means there are ten different relationships. These ten distinctive relationships are known as the Ten Gods.

Power

The element that controls the Day Stem is known as Power. For a Yang Wood or Yin Wood Day Stem, it is controlled by Metal. Metal is Power for Yang Wood and Yin Wood Day Stems.

The Power that is of the opposite polarity as the Day Stem is the Direct Power. The Power that is of the same polarity as the Day Stem is the Seven Killings.

For a Yang Wood Day Stem, Yin Metal is of the opposite polarity. This makes Yin Metal the Direct Power. Yang Metal is of the same polarity as Yang Wood. Yang Metal is the Seven Killings.

For a Yin Wood Day Stem, Yang Metal is of the opposite polarity. Yang Metal is the Direct Power. Yin Metal is of the same polarity. Yin Metal is the Seven Killings.

Table 1.1 lists the Day Stem with the corresponding Direct Power and Seven Killings.

Table 1.1 Day Stem with Direct Power and Seven Killings

Day Stem	Direct Power	Seven Killings
甲 Yang Wood	辛 Yin Metal	庚 Yang Metal
乙 Yin Wood	庚 Yang Metal	辛 Yin Metal
丙 Yang Fire	癸 Yin Water	壬 Yang Water
丁 Yin Fire	壬 Yang Water	癸 Yin Water
戊 Yang Earth	乙 Yin Wood	甲 Yang Wood
己 Yin Earth	甲 Yang Wood	乙 Yin Wood
庚 Yang Metal	丁 Yin Fire	丙 Yang Fire
辛 Yin Metal	丙 Yang Fire	丁 Yin Fire
壬 Yang Water	己 Yin Earth	戊 Yang Earth
癸 Yin Water	戊 Yang Earth	己 Yin Earth

Output

The element that the Day Stem produces is known as Output. For a Yang Fire or Yin Fire Day Stem, the element that is produced is Earth. Earth is Output for Yang Fire and Yin Fire.

The Output that is of the same polarity as the Day Stem is known as the Eating God. The Output that is of the opposite polarity as the Day Stem is the Seven Killings.

For a Yang Fire Day Stem, Yang Earth is of the same polarity. Yang Earth is the Eating God. Yin Earth is of the opposite polarity. Yin Earth is the Hurting Officer.

For a Yin Fire Day Stem, Yin Earth is of the same polarity. Yin Earth is the Eating God. Yang Earth is of the opposite polarity. Yang Earth is the Hurting Officer.

Table 1.2 lists the Day Stem with the corresponding Eating God and Hurting Officer.

Table 1.2 Day Stem with Eating God and Hurting Officer

Day Stem	Eating God	Hurting Officer
甲 Yang Wood	丙 Yang Fire	丁 Yin Fire
乙 Yin Wood	丁 Yin Fire	丙 Yang Fire
丙 Yang Fire	戊 Yang Earth	己 Yin Earth
丁 Yin Fire	己 Yin Earth	戊 Yang Earth
戊 Yang Earth	庚 Yang Metal	辛 Yin Metal
己 Yin Earth	辛 Yin Metal	庚 Yang Metal
庚 Yang Metal	壬 Yang Water	癸 Yin Water
辛 Yin Metal	癸 Yin Water	壬 Yang Water
壬 Yang Water	甲 Yang Wood	乙 Yin Wood
癸 Yin Water	乙 Yin Wood	甲 Yang Wood

Wealth

The element that the Day Stem controls is Wealth. For a Yang Earth or Yin Earth Day Stem, the element that is controlled is Water. Water is Wealth for Yang Earth and Yin Earth Day Stems.

The Wealth that is of the opposite polarity as the Day Stem is the Direct Wealth. The Wealth that is of the same polarity as the Day Stem is the Indirect Wealth.

For a Yang Earth Day Stem, Yin Water is of the opposite

polarity. Yin Water is the Direct Wealth. Yang Water is of the same polarity. Yang Water is the Indirect Wealth.

For a Yin Earth Day Stem, Yang Water is of the opposite polarity. Yang Water is the Direct Wealth. Yin Water is of the same polarity. Yin Water is the Indirect Wealth.

Table 1.3 lists the Day Stem with the corresponding Direct Wealth and Indirect Wealth.

Table 1.3 Day Stem with Direct Wealth and Indirect Wealth

Day Stem	Direct Wealth	Indirect Wealth
甲 Yang Wood	己 Yin Earth	戊 Yang Earth
乙 Yin Wood	戊 Yang Earth	己 Yin Earth
丙 Yang Fire	辛 Yin Metal	庚 Yang Metal
丁 Yin Fire	庚 Yang Metal	辛 Yin Metal
戊 Yang Earth	癸 Yin Water	壬 Yang Water
己 Yin Earth	壬 Yang Water	癸 Yin Water
庚 Yang Metal	乙 Yin Wood	甲 Yang Wood
辛 Yin Metal	甲 Yang Wood	乙 Yin Wood
壬 Yang Water	丁 Yin Fire	丙 Yang Fire
癸 Yin Water	丙 Yang Fire	丁 Yin Fire

Resource

The element that produces the Day Stem is Resource. For a Yang Metal or Yin Metal Day Stem, the element that produces it is the Earth. Earth is Resource for Yang Metal and Yin Metal Day Stems.

The Resource that is of the opposite polarity is the Direct Resource. The Resource that is of the same polarity is the Indirect Resource.

For a Yang Metal Day Stem, Yin Earth is of the opposite polarity. Yin Earth is the Direct Resource. Yang Earth is of the same polarity. Yang Earth is the Indirect Resource.

For a Yin Metal Day Stem, Yang Earth is of the opposite polarity. Yang Earth is the Direct Resource. Yin Earth is of the same polarity. Yin Earth is the Indirect Resource.

Table 1.4 lists the Day Stem with the corresponding Direct Resource and Indirect Resource.

Table 1.4 Day Stem with Direct Resource and Indirect Resource

Day Stem	Direct Resource	Indirect Resource
甲 Yang Wood	癸 Yin Water	壬 Yang Water
乙 Yin Wood	壬 Yang Water	癸 Yin Water
丙 Yang Fire	乙 Yin Wood	甲 Yang Wood
丁 Yin Fire	甲 Yang Wood	乙 Yin Wood
戊 Yang Earth	丁 Yin Fire	丙 Yang Fire
己 Yin Earth	丙 Yang Fire	丁 Yin Fire
庚 Yang Metal	己 Yin Earth	戊 Yang Earth
辛 Yin Metal	戊 Yang Earth	己 Yin Earth
壬 Yang Water	辛 Yin Metal	庚 Yang Metal
癸 Yin Water	庚 Yang Metal	辛 Yin Metal

Rival

The element that is of the same element as the Day Stem is the Rival. For a Yang Water or Yin Water Day Stem, the element that is the same is Water. Water is the Rival for Yang Water and Yin Water Day Stems.

The Rival that is of the same polarity is Sibling. The Rival that is of the opposite polarity is Rob Wealth.

For a Yang Water Day Stem, Yang Water is of the same polarity. Yang Water is Sibling. Yin Water is of the opposite polarity. Yin Water is Rob Wealth.

For a Yin Water Day Stem, Yin Water is of the same polarity. Yin Water is Sibling. Yang Water is of the opposite polarity. Yang Water is Rob Wealth.

Table 1.5 lists the Day Stem with corresponding Sibling and Rob Wealth.

1.5 Day Stem with Sibling and Rob Wealth

Day Stem	Sibling	Rob Wealth
甲 Yang Wood	甲 Yang Wood	乙 Yin Wood
乙 Yin Wood	乙 Yin Wood	甲 Yang Wood
丙 Yang Fire	丙 Yang Fire	丁 Yin Fire
丁 Yin Fire	丁 Yin Fire	丙 Yang Fire
戊 Yang Earth	戊 Yang Earth	己 Yin Earth
己 Yin Earth	己 Yin Earth	戊 Yang Earth
庚 Yang Metal	庚 Yang Metal	辛 Yin Metal
辛 Yin Metal	辛 Yin Metal	庚 Yang Metal
壬 Yang Water	壬 Yang Water	癸 Yin Water
癸 Yin Water	癸 Yin Water	壬 Yang Water

Hidden Stems

Within the Branches, there are Stems that are hidden in it.

Table 1.6 lists the hidden Stems that are present within the Branches, ranking them in order of importance.

Table 1.6 12 Branches with hidden Stems

Branch	Hidden Stems
子 Rat	癸 Yin Water
丑 Ox	己 Yin Earth 辛 Yin Metal 癸 Yin Water
寅 Tiger	丙 Yang Fire 甲 Yang Wood 戊 Yang Earth
卯 Rabbit	乙 Yin Wood
辰 Dragon	戊 Yang Earth 癸 Yin Water 乙 Yin Wood
巳 Snake	庚 Yang Metal 丙 Yang Fire 戊 Yang Earth
午 Horse	丁 Yin Fire 己 Yin Earth
未 Sheep	己 Yin Earth 乙 Yin Wood 丁 Yin Fire
申 Monkey	壬 Yang Water 庚 Yang Metal 戊 Yang Earth
酉 Rooster	辛 Yin Metal
戌 Dog	戊 Yang Earth 丁 Yin Fire
亥 Pig	甲 Yang Wood 壬 Yang Water

Note that for three of the four Peak Branches, i.e. Rat, Rabbit and Rooster, there is only one hidden Stem. This is because these Branches are the Peak of the Three Harmony and Seasonal Combination of the same element. For example, the Rat is the Peak of the Three Harmony Water Combination (see Table 1.8) and Seasonal Water Combination (see Table 1.9). For the Horse, there are two, i.e. Fire and Earth. This is because Earth does not have its own Three Harmony Combination and is associated with Fire.

For the Earth Branches i.e. Ox, Dragon, Sheep and Dog, the prevalent element is Earth. For Dragon and Dog, the most important Stem is Yang Earth. For Ox and Sheep, the most important Stem is Yin Earth. For the Earth Branches, the second hidden Stem would be that associated with the Three Harmony Combination (see Table 1.8). The third hidden Stem is that associated with the Seasonal Combination (see Table 1.9).

For the Birth Branches, i.e. Tiger, Snake, Monkey and Pig, the prevalent hidden Stem is that associated with the Three Harmony Combination (see Table 1.8). The second hidden Stem is that associated with the Seasonal Combination (see Table 1.9). There is also Earth present in the Tiger, Snake and Monkey but not the Pig.

Table 1.7 lists the hidden Stems associated with the Branches, dividing them into the Three Harmony Combination, Seasonal Combination and Earth. Table 1.8 lists the Three Harmony Combinations, while Table 1.9 lists the Seasonal Combinations.

Table 1.7 12 Branches and hidden Stems with classification

Day Stem	Three Harmony	Earth	Seasonal
子 Rat	癸 Yin Water		
丑 Ox	辛 Yin Metal	己 Yin Earth	癸 Yin Water
寅 Tiger	丙 Yang Fire	戊 Yang Earth	甲 Yang Wood
卯 Rabbit	乙 Yin Wood		
辰 Dragon	癸 Yin Water	戊 Yang Earth	乙 Yin Wood
巳 Snake	庚 Yang Metal	戊 Yang Earth	丙 Yang Fire
午 Horse	丁 Yin Fire	己 Yin Earth	
未 Sheep	乙 Yin Wood	己 Yin Earth	丁 Yin Fire

申 Monkey	壬 Yang Water	戊 Yang Earth	庚 Yang Metal
酉 Rooster	辛 Yin Metal		
戌 Dog	丁 Yin Fire	戊 Yang Earth	辛 Yin Metal
亥 Pig	甲 Yang Wood		壬 Yang Water

Table 1.8 Element and Three Harmony Combination

Element	Three Harmony Combination
Water	申 Monkey 子 Rat 辰 Dragon
Wood	亥 Pig 卯 Rabbit 未 Sheep
Fire	寅 Tiger 午 Horse 戌 Dog
Metal	巳 Snake 酉 Rooster 丑 Ox

Table 1.9 Element and Seasonal Combination

Element	Three Harmony Combination
Water	亥 Pig 子 Rat 丑 Ox
Wood	寅 Tiger 卯 Rabbit 辰 Dragon
Fire	巳 Snake 午 Horse 未 Sheep
Metal	申 Monkey 酉 Rooster 戌 Dog

The hidden Stems within the Branches are related to the Day Stem to ascertain the associated Ten Gods.

貳

Chapter Two

Chapter Two Direct Power

The Power element is the element that controls the Self element. For example, in the Cycle of Control, Metal controls Wood. Therefore, for Yang Wood and Yin Wood Day Stems, the Power element is Metal.

Direct Power refers to the Power element that is of the opposite polarity of the Day Master. For Yang Wood, Yin Metal represents Direct Power. For Yin Wood, Yang Metal represents Direct Power.

The Direct Power can be present in the Stems or hidden in the Branches in the Four Pillars chart.

Table 2.1 lists the Day Stem and the corresponding Direct Power.

Table 2.1 Day Stem and Direct Power

Day Stem	Direct Power
甲 Yang Wood	辛 Yin Metal
乙 Yin Wood	庚 Yang Metal
丙 Yang Fire	癸 Yin Water
丁 Yin Fire	壬 Yang Water
戊 Yang Earth	乙 Yin Wood
己 Yin Earth	甲 Yang Wood
庚 Yang Metal	丁 Yin Fire
辛 Yin Metal	丙 Yang Fire
壬 Yang Water	己 Yin Earth
癸 Yin Water	戊 Yang Earth

Note that for Yin Day Stems, the Direct Power combines with them. For instance, Yang Earth (Direct Power) combines with the Yin Water Day Stem. For the Yin Metal Day Stem, Yang Fire (Direct Power) combines with it.

The presence of the Direct Power in the chart indicates a person who sits quietly and securely. Direct Power that is hidden in the Branches is also considered.

Direct Power on the Nobleman

The Direct Power on the Nobleman Pillar can be present in the Year, Month or Hour within the chart.

Table 2.2 lists the Nobleman Stars for all Day Stems. Note that some of the Stems share the same Nobleman Stars.

Table 2.2 Day Stems and Nobleman Stars

Day Stems	Nobleman Stars
甲 Yang Wood 戊 Yang Earth 庚 Yang Metal	丑 Ox 未 Sheep
乙 Yin Wood 己 Yin Earth	子 Rat 申 Monkey
丙 Yang Fire 丁 Yin Fire	酉 Rooster 亥 Pig
辛 Yin Metal	寅 Tiger 午 Horse
壬 Yang Water 癸 Yin Water	卯 Rabbit 巳 Snake

When the Direct Power sits on a Nobleman Star (as determined by the Day Stem), it indicates that the person will be successful. They enjoy a good career. For women, there is the possibility of marrying a good husband.

Table 2.3 lists the Direct Power Sitting on the Nobleman Pillar for all Day Stems.

Table 2.3 Day Stem and Direct Power Sitting on the Nobleman Pillars

Day Stems	Direct Power Sitting on Nobleman	Direct Power Sitting on Nobleman
甲 Yang Wood	辛 Yin Metal 丑 Ox	**辛 Yin Metal 未 Sheep**
乙 Yin Wood	庚 Yang Metal 子 Rat	庚 Yang Metal 申 Monkey
丙 Yang Fire	癸 Yin Water 酉 Rooster	癸 Yin Water 亥 Pig
丁 Yin Fire		
戊 Yang Earth	乙 Yin Wood 丑 Ox	乙 Yin Wood 未 Sheep
己 Yin Earth	**甲 Yang Wood 子 Rat**	甲 Yang Wood 申 Monkey
庚 Yang Metal	**丁 Yin Fire 丑 Ox**	丁 Yin Fire 未 Sheep
辛 Yin Metal	丙 Yang Fire 寅 Tiger	丙 Yang Fire 午 Horse
壬 Yang Water	己 Yin Earth 卯 Rabbit	己 Yin Earth 巳 Snake
癸 Yin Water		

Only the Pillars that are in bold can appear in the Hour Pillars.

Note that Yin Fire and Yin Water do not have any Direct Power on the Nobleman Pillars. The Nobleman Branch always has the same polarity as the Direct Power.

For Yin Fire, the Direct Power is Yang Water. The Nobleman Branches for Yin Fire are Rooster and Pig. Both Branches are of the Yin polarity.

For Yin Water, the Direct Power is Yang Earth. The Nobleman Branches for Yin Water are the Rabbit and Snake, which are of the Yin polarity.

The following examples illustrate each of the Direct Power Nobleman Pillars.

Example 2.1

Susan Boyle, Scottish Singer, April 1, 1961, 09:50 hours DST

Hour	Day	Month	Year
戊	甲	辛	辛
Yang Earth	**Yang Wood**	Yin Metal	**Yin Metal**
辰	子	卯	丑
Dragon	Rat	Rabbit	**Ox**

Boyle is a Yang Wood Day Stem. The Direct Power on the Nobleman Pillar Yin Metal Ox is present in the Year. In 2009 (Yin Earth Ox year), she rose to fame as a contestant on *Britain's Got Talent*. Boyle's debut studio album, *I Dreamed a Dream*, became the UK's best-selling debut album of all time.

Example 2.2

Jessica Simpson, American Singer and Actress
July 10, 1980, 15:11 hours DST

Hour	Day	Month	Year
辛	甲	壬	庚
Yin Metal	**Yang Wood**	Yang Water	Yang Metal
未	申	午	申
Sheep	Monkey	Horse	Monkey

Simpson is a Yang Wood Day Stem. The Direct Power on the Nobleman Pillar Yin Metal Sheep is present in the Hour. Not only is Simpson a singer and actress, she also has her own line of clothing, *The Jessica Simpson Collection*, which has earned more than 1 billion USD.

Example 2.3

Billie Eilish, American Singer-Songwriter
December 18, 2001, 11:30 hours

Hour	Day	Month	Year
壬	乙	庚	辛
Yang Water	**Yin Wood**	**Yang Metal**	Yin Metal
午	卯	子	巳
Horse	Rabbit	**Rat**	Snake

Eilish is a Yin Wood Day Stem. The Direct Power on the Nobleman Pillar Yang Metal Rat is present in the Month. In 2020 (Yang Metal Rat year), she became the youngest artist ever to win Best New Artist, Record, Song and Album at the Grammy Awards in the same year.

Example 2.4

Coco Chanel, French Fashion Designer
August 19, 1883, 16:00 hours

Hour	Day	Month	Year
甲	乙	庚	癸
Yang Wood	**Yin Wood**	**Yang Metal**	Yin Water
申	未	申	未
Monkey	Sheep	**Monkey**	Sheep

Chanel is a Yin Wood Day Stem. The Direct Power on the Nobleman Pillar Yang Metal Monkey is present in the Month. She was the founder and namesake of the *Chanel* brand. Her signature scent, *Chanel No. 5*, has become iconic.

Example 2.5

Lindsey Buckingham, American Musician and Singer
Fleetwood Mac, October 3, 1949, 01:53 hours

Hour	Day	Month	Year
己	丙	癸	己
Yin Earth	**Yang Fire**	**Yin Water**	Yin Earth
丑	寅	酉	丑
Ox	Tiger	**Rooster**	Ox

Buckingham is a Yang Fire Day Stem. The Direct Power on the Nobleman Pillar Yin Water Rooster is present in the Month. He was the lead vocalist and guitarist of the best-selling music group *Fleetwood Mac*.

Example 2.6

Donald Glover, American Actor and Musician
September 25, 1983, 05:56 hours DST

Hour	Day	Month	Year
庚	丙	辛	癸
Yang Metal	**Yang Fire**	Yin Metal	**Yin Water**
寅	辰	酉	亥
Tiger	Dragon	Rooster	**Pig**

Glover is a Yang Fire Day Stem. The Direct Power on the Nobleman Pillar Yin Water Pig is present in the Year. An actor, singer and writer, he has won two Emmys, two Golden Globes and Four Grammys.

Example 2.7

Harry Styles, English Singer-Songwriter and Actor *One Direction,* February 1, 1994, 00:06 hours

Hour	Day	Month	Year
壬	戊	乙	癸
Yang Water	**Yang Earth**	**Yin Wood**	Yin Water
子	午	丑	酉
Rat	Horse	**Ox**	Rooster

Styles is a Yang Earth Day Stem. His Direct Power on the Nobleman Pillar Yin Wood Ox is present in the Month. Following his years with the best selling group *One Direction,* he released three solo albums, all of which reached Number One on the US or UK Albums charts.

Example 2.8

Kristi Yamaguchi, American Figure Skater
July 12, 1971, 09:02 hours DST

Hour	Day	Month	Year
丙	戊	乙	辛
Yang Fire	**Yang Earth**	**Yin Wood**	Yin Metal
辰	戌	未	亥
Dragon	Dog	**Sheep**	Pig

Yamaguchi is a Yang Earth Day Stem. The Direct Power on the Nobleman Pillar Yin Wood Sheep is present in the Month. She became the first Asian American woman to win a Winter Olympics Gold Medal in 1992 (Yang Water Monkey year).

Example 2.9

Queen Elizabeth the Queen Mother, British Royalty
August 4, 1900, 00:30 hours

Hour	Day	Month	Year
甲	己	甲	庚
Yang Wood	**Yin Earth**	**Yang Wood**	Yang Metal
子	酉	申	子
Rat	Rooster	**Monkey**	Rat

The Queen Mother is a Yin Earth Day Stem. Both the Direct Power on the Nobleman Pillars Yang Wood Rat and Yang Wood Monkey are present in the Hour and Month respectively. She was a consistently popular member of the British Royal Family and appeared in public life until a few months before her death in 2002 (Yang Water Horse year) at the age of 101.

Example 2.10

Carlos Santana, Mexican-American Guitarist
July 20, 1947, 02:00 hours

Hour	Day	Month	Year
丁	庚	丁	丁
Yin Fire	**Yang Metal**	**Yin Fire**	Yin Fire
丑	子	未	亥
Ox	Rat	**Sheep**	Pig

Santana is a Yang Metal Day Stem. Both Direct Power on the Nobleman Pillars, Yin Fire Ox and Yin Fire Sheep are present in the Hour and Month respectively. He has won ten Grammy Awards and was inducted into the Rock and Roll Hall of Fame in 1998 (Yang Earth Tiger year).

Example 2.11

Ivana Trump, American Businesswoman and Model
February 20, 1949, 00:55 hours

Hour	Day	Month	Year
戊	辛	丙	己
Yang Earth	**Yin Metal**	**Yang Fire**	Yin Earth
子	巳	寅	丑
Rat	Snake	**Tiger**	Ox

Trump is a Yin Metal Day Stem. The Direct Power on the Nobleman Pillar Yang Fire Tiger is present in the Month. Following her divorce from her husband Donald, she has developed her own lines of clothing, fashion, jewellery and beauty products.

Example 2.12

Gordon Ramsay, British Chef and Restaurateur
November 8, 1966, 18:05 hours

Hour	Day	Month	Year
丁	辛	戊	丙
Yin Fire	**Yin Metal**	Yang Earth	**Yang Fire**
酉	未	戌	午
Rooster	Sheep	Dog	**Horse**

Ramsay is a Yin Metal Day Stem. The Direct Power on Nobleman Pillar Yang Fire Horse is present in the Year. Ramsay became known for the television series *Boiling Point* in 1999 (Yin Earth Rabbit year). He is one of the most influential and well-known chefs in the United Kingdom.

Example 2.13

Sir Ian McKellen, English Actor
May 25, 1939, 21:30 hours

Hour	Day	Month	Year
辛	壬	己	己
Yin Metal	**Yang Water**	**Yin Earth**	**Yin Earth**
亥	戌	巳	卯
Pig	Dog	**Snake**	**Rabbit**

McKellen is a Yang Water Day Stem. Both Direct Power on the Nobleman Pillars Yin Earth Rabbit and Yin Earth Snake are present in the Year and Month respectively. He is a recipient of every major theatrical award in the UK and is regarded as a British cultural icon.

Direct Power as a Solar or Lunar Helper

When the Direct Power is also a Solar or Lunar Helper, present in the Month Pillar, then the person will be successful and a high achiever.

The Solar and Lunar Helpers are derived from the Month Branch of birth. Table 2.4 lists the Month Branches and the corresponding Solar and Lunar Helper.

Table 2.4 Month Branches with Solar and Lunar Helpers

Month Branch	Solar Helper	Lunar Helper
子 Rat	巳 Snake	壬 Yang Water
丑 Ox	庚 Yang Metal	庚 Yang Metal
寅 Tiger	丁 Yin Fire	丙 Yang Fire
卯 Rabbit	申 Monkey	甲 Yang Wood

辰 Dragon	壬 Yang Water	壬 Yang Water
巳 Snake	辛 Yin Metal	庚 Yang Metal
午 Horse	亥 Pig	丙 Yang Fire
未 Sheep	甲 Yang Wood	甲 Yang Wood
申 Monkey	癸 Yin Water	壬 Yang Water
酉 Rooster	寅 Tiger	庚 Yang Metal
戌 Dog	丙 Yang Fire	丙 Yang Fire
亥 Pig	乙 Yin Wood	甲 Yang Wood

As the Month Branch determines the Solar and Lunar Helpers, we will only consider the Month Pillar for Direct Power as a Solar or Lunar Helper.

Taking into account that the Month Branch and the Solar or Lunar Helper must be of the same polarity, there are only eight of these Month Pillars to consider.

Table 2.5 lists the six Direct Power as Lunar Helper Pillars and the two Direct Power as Solar Helper as Solar Helper Pillars and the corresponding Stem.

Table 2.5 Day Stem and Direct Power as Solar or Lunar Helpers

Day Stem	Direct Power as Solar or Lunar Helper
甲 Yang Wood	辛 Yin Metal (Solar) 巳 Snake
丁 Yin Fire	壬 Yang Water 壬 Yang Water 壬 Yang Water (Lunar) 申 Monkey　　子 Rat　　　辰 Dragon
戊 Yang Earth	乙 Yin Wood (Solar) 亥 Pig
辛 Yin Metal	丙 Yang Fire 丙 Yang Fire 丙 Yang Fire (Lunar) 寅 Tiger　　午 Horse　　戌 Dog

The following examples list each of the Direct Power as a Solar or Lunar Helper.

Example 2.14

Dana Carvey, American Actor and Comedian
June 2, 1955, 12:00 hours

Hour	Day	Month	Year
庚	甲	辛	乙
Yang Metal	**Yang Wood**	**Yin Metal**	Yin Wood
午	午	巳	未
Horse	Horse	**Snake**	Sheep

Carvey is a Yang Wood Day Stem. He is born in the Snake Month, with Yin Metal as the Solar Helper. The Direct Power as a Solar Helper, Yin Metal Snake is present in the Month. Carvey is a comedian known for his seven seasons on *Saturday Night Live* from 1986 (Yang Fire Tiger year) to 1993 (Yin Water Rooster year).

Example 2.15

Gene Simmons, Israeli-American Singer-Songwriter *KISS*
August 25, 1949, 10:15 hours

Hour	Day	Month	Year
乙	丁	壬	己
Yin Wood	**Yin Fire**	**Yang Water**	Yin Earth
巳	亥	申	丑
Snake	Pig	**Monkey**	Ox

Simmons is a Yin Fire Day Stem. He is born in the Monkey Month, with Yang Water as the Lunar Helper. The Direct Power as a Lunar Helper, Yang Water Monkey is present in the Month. Simmons is the co-lead singer of *KISS*, which has sold more than 100 million records worldwide.

Example 2.16

Dilma Rousseff, President of Brazil 2011 to 2016
December 14, 1947, 02:00 hours

Hour	Day	Month	Year
辛	丁	壬	丁
Yin Metal	**Yin Fire**	**Yang Water**	Yin Fire
丑	卯	子	亥
Ox	Rabbit	**Rat**	Pig

Rousseff is a Yin Fire Day Stem. She is born in the Rat Month, with Yang Water as the Lunar Helper. The Direct Power as a Lunar Helper, Yang Water Rat is present in the Month. Rousseff was the first woman to be President of Brazil, from 2011 (Yin Metal Rabbit year) to 2016 (Yang Fire Monkey year).

Example 2.17

Harper Lee, American Novelist
April 28, 1926, 17:25 hours

Hour	Day	Month	Year
己	丁	壬	丙
Yin Earth	**Yin Fire**	**Yang Water**	Yang Fire
酉	亥	辰	寅
Rooster	Pig	**Dragon**	Tiger

Lee is a Yin Fire Day Stem. She is born in the Dragon Month, with Yang Water as the Solar and Lunar Helper. The Direct Power as a Solar and Lunar Helper, Yang Water Dragon is present in the Month. In 1961 (Yin Metal Ox year), Lee won the Pulitzer Prize for her novel *To Kill a Mockingbird*.

Example 2.18

Rickie Lee Jones, American Singer,
November 8, 1954, 05:50 hours

Hour	Day	Month	Year
丁	戊	乙	甲
Yin Fire	**Yang Earth**	**Yin Wood**	Yang Wood
卯	辰	亥	午
Rabbit	Dragon	**Pig**	Horse

Jones is a Yang Earth Day Stem. She is born in the Pig Month, with Yin Wood as a Solar Helper. The Direct Power as a Solar Helper, Yin Wood Pig is present in the Month. Jones has enjoyed a five-decade career and has won two Grammy Awards.

Example 2.19

John McEnroe, American Tennis Player,
February 18, 1959, 22:30 hours

Hour	Day	Month	Year
己	辛	丙	己
Yin Earth	**Yin Metal**	**Yang Fire**	Yin Earth
亥	未	寅	亥
Pig	Sheep	**Tiger**	Pig

McEnroe is a Yin Metal Day Stem. He is born in the Tiger Month, with Yang Fire as the Lunar Helper. The Direct Power as a Lunar Helper, Yang Fire Tiger is present in the Month. Note that the Yang Fire Tiger Month is also a Direct Power on the Nobleman Pillar.

Example 2.20

Jean Dujardin, French Actor, June 19, 1972, 04:50 hours

Hour	Day	Month	Year
庚	辛	丙	壬
Yang Metal	**Yin Metal**	**Yang Fire**	Yang Water
寅	巳	午	子
Tiger	Snake	**Horse**	Rat

Dujardin is a Yin Metal Day Stem. He is born in the Horse Month, with Yang Fire as the Lunar Helper. The Direct Power as a Lunar Helper, Yang Fire Tiger is present in the Month. Note that the Yang Fire Horse Month is also a Direct Power on the Nobleman Pillar. He became the first French actor to win the Oscar for Best Actor for *The Artist* in 2012 (Yang Water Dragon year).

Example 2.21

Matt Damon, American Actor, October 8, 1970, 15:22 hours DST

Hour	Day	Month	Year
乙	辛	丙	庚
Yin Wood	**Yin Metal**	**Yang Fire**	Yang Metal
未	酉	戌	戌
Sheep	Rooster	**Dog**	Dog

Damon is a Yin Metal Day Stem. He is born in the Dog Month, with Yang Fire as both the Solar and Lunar Helper. The Direct Power as a Solar and Lunar Helper, Yang Fire Dog is present in the Month. Damon's movies have grossed more than USD 3.88 billion at the North American box office.

Direct Power on the Academic Star

When the Direct Power is sitting on an Academic star, the person is cultured, well behaved and enjoys reading. They will enjoy a good position and fame.

Table 2.6 lists all the Stems with the corresponding Academic Star and Direct Power.

Table 2.6 Day Stem with Academic Star and Direct Power

Day Stem	Academic Star	Direct Power
甲 Yang Wood	巳 Snake	辛 Yin Metal
乙 Yin Wood	午 Horse	庚 Yang Metal
丙 Yang Fire	申 Monkey	癸 Yin Water
丁 Yin Fire	酉 Rooster	壬 Yang Water
戊 Yang Earth	申 Monkey	乙 Yin Wood
己 Yin Earth	酉 Rooster	甲 Yang Wood
庚 Yang Metal	亥 Pig	丁 Yin Fire
辛 Yin Metal	子 Rat	丙 Yang Fire
壬 Yang Water	寅 Tiger	己 Yin Earth
癸 Yin Water	卯 Rabbit	戊 Yang Earth

For the Direct Power on the Academic Star Pillar, they have to be of the same polarity. This is only applicable to four Day Stems.

Table 2.7 lists the Day Stem and Direct Power on the Academic Star Pillar with the same polarity.

Table 2.7 Day Stem and Direct Power on the Academic Star Pillars

Day Stem	Direct Power On the Academic Star
甲 Yang Wood	辛 Yin Metal 巳 Snake
乙 Yin Wood	庚 Yang Metal 午 Horse
庚 Yang Metal	**丁 Yin Fire** **亥 Pig**
辛 Yin Metal	丙 Yang Fire 子 Rat

The Yin Fire Pig Pillar can also appear in the Hour Pillar.

The following examples illustrate each of the Direct Power on the Academic Star pillars.

Example 2.22

Paul Simon, American Singer and Musician, October 13, 1941, 02:33 hours

Hour	Day	Month	Year
乙	甲	丁	辛
Yin Wood	**Yang Wood**	Yin Fire	**Yin Metal**
丑	午	酉	巳
Ox	Horse	Rooster	**Snake**

Simon is a Yang Wood Day Stem. The Direct Power on the Academic Star Pillar Yin Metal Snake is present in the Year. He has enjoyed a six-decade career and is one of the most acclaimed songwriters in popular music.

Example 2.23

Courteney Cox, American Actress,
June 15, 1964, 17:30 hours DST

Hour	Day	Month	Year
甲	乙	庚	甲
Yang Wood	**Yin Wood**	**Yang Metal**	Yang Wood
申	未	午	辰
Monkey	Sheep	**Horse**	Dragon

Cox is a Yin Wood Day Stem. The Direct Power on the Academic Star Pillar Yang Metal Horse is present in the Month. She gained international recognition for her role in the television series *Friends*, which ran from 1994 (Yang Wood Dog year) to 2004 (Yang Wood Monkey year).

Example 2.24

Jessica Chastain, American Actress,
March 24, 1977, 22:44 hours

Hour	Day	Month	Year
丁	庚	癸	丁
Yin Fire	**Yang Metal**	Yin Water	Yin Fire
亥	辰	卯	巳
Pig	Dragon	Rabbit	Snake

Chastain is a Yang Metal Day Stem. The Direct Power on the Academic Star Pillar Yin Fire Pig is present in the Hour. Chastain won an Oscar for Best Actress for her performance in *The Eyes of Tammy Faye* in 2022 (Yang Water Tiger year).

Example 2.25

Arnold Schwarzenegger, Austrian-American Actor and Politician, July 30, 1947, 04:10 hours

Hour	Day	Month	Year
戊	**庚**	丁	丁
Yang Earth	**Yang Metal**	Yin Fire	**Yin Fire**
寅	戌	未	亥
Tiger	Dog	Sheep	**Pig**

Schwarzenegger is a Yang Metal Day Stem. The Direct Power on the Academic Star Pillar Yin Fire Pig is present in the Year. Note that the Direct Power on the Nobleman Pillar Yin Fire Sheep is also present in the Month. Not only is Schwarzenegger a Hollywood action star, he was also the Governor of California from 2003 (Yin Water Sheep year) to 2011 (Yin Metal Rabbit year).

Example 2.26

Bradley Cooper, American Actor and Filmmaker, January 5, 1975, 05:09 hours

Hour	Day	Month	Year
辛	**辛**	丙	甲
Yin Metal	**Yin Metal**	**Yang Fire**	Yang Wood
卯	亥	子	寅
Rabbit	Pig	**Rat**	Tiger

Cooper is a Yin Metal Day Stem. The Direct Power on the Academic Star Pillar Yang Fire Rat is present in the Month. He has received a British Academy Film Award and two Grammy Awards.

Direct Power on the Prosperity Pillar

When the Direct Power is sitting on the Prosperity Life Stage (as determined by the Three Harmony Life Stages), then there is professional recognition and success. There are five Direct Power Yang Stems and five Direct Power Yin Stems to consider.

The Direct Power is the opposite polarity of the Day Stem. For Yin Day Stems, consider Table 2.8 and for Yang Day Stems, look up Table 2.9.

Table 2.8 lists the 12 Life Stages for the Direct Power Yang Stems. The Life Stages to take into account are the Arrival and Peak, which have been highlighted.

Table 2.8 12 Life Stages for the Direct Power Yang Stems

Stem Life Stage	甲 Yang Wood	丙 Yang Fire	戊 Yang Earth	庚 Yang Metal	壬 Yang Water
Birth	亥 Pig	寅 Tiger	寅 Tiger	巳 Snake	申 Monkey
Bath	子 Rat	卯 Rabbit	卯 Rabbit	午 Horse	酉 Rooster
Attire	丑 Ox	辰 Dragon	辰 Dragon	未 Sheep	戌 Dog
Arrival	**寅 Tiger**	巳 Snake	巳 Snake	**申 Monkey**	亥 Pig
Peak	卯 Rabbit	**午 Horse**	**午 Horse**	酉 Rooster	**子 Rat**
Ageing	辰 Dragon	未 Sheep	未 Sheep	戌 Dog	丑 Ox
Sickness	巳 Snake	申 Monkey	申 Monkey	亥 Pig	寅 Tiger
Death	午 Horse	酉 Rooster	酉 Rooster	子 Rat	卯 Rabbit

Tomb	未 Sheep	戌 Dog	戌 Dog	丑 Ox	辰 Dragon
End	申 Monkey	亥 Pig	亥 Pig	寅 Tiger	巳 Snake
Conception	酉 Rooster	子 Rat	子 Rat	卯 Rabbit	午 Horse
Nurture	戌 Dog	丑 Ox	丑 Ox	辰 Dragon	未 Sheep

Table 2.9 lists the 12 Life Stages for Direct Power Yin Stems. The Life Stages to take into account are the Peak and Arrival, which have been highlighted.

Table 2.9 12 Life Stages for the Direct Power Yin Stems

Stem Life Stage	乙 Yin Wood	丁 Yin Fire	己 Yin Earth	辛 Yin Metal	癸 Yin Water
Birth	午 Horse	酉 Rooster	酉 Rooster	子 Rat	卯 Rabbit
Bath	巳 Snake	申 Monkey	申 Monkey	亥 Pig	寅 Tiger
Attire	辰 Dragon	未 Sheep	未 Sheep	戌 Dog	丑 Ox
Arrival	卯 **Rabbit**	午 Horse	午 Horse	酉 **Rooster**	子 Rat
Peak	寅 Tiger	巳 **Snake**	巳 **Snake**	申 Monkey	亥 **Pig**
Ageing	丑 Ox	辰 Dragon	辰 Dragon	未 Sheep	戌 Dog
Sickness	子 Rat	卯 Rabbit	卯 Rabbit	午 Horse	酉 Rooster
Death	亥 Pig	寅 Tiger	寅 Tiger	巳 Snake	申 Monkey
Tomb	戌 Dog	丑 Ox	丑 Ox	辰 Dragon	未 Sheep
End	酉 Rooster	子 Rat	子 Rat	卯 Rabbit	午 Horse

| Concep-tion | 申 Monkey | 亥 Pig | 亥 Pig | 寅 Tiger | 巳 Snake |
| Nurture | 未 Sheep | 戌 Dog | 戌 Dog | 丑 Ox | 辰 Dragon |

Table 2.10 lists the Stems with the Direct Power On the Prosperity Pillar.

Table 2.10 Day Stem with Direct Power on the Prosperity Pillar

Stem	Direct Power on the Prosperity Pillar
甲 Yang Wood	辛 Yin Metal 酉 Rooster
乙 Yin Wood	庚 Yang Metal 申 Monkey
丙 Yang Fire	癸 Yin Water 亥 Pig
丁 Yin Fire	壬 Yang Water 子 Rat
戊 Yang Earth	**乙 Yin Wood** **卯 Rabbit**
己 Yin Earth	甲 Yang Wood 寅 Tiger
庚 Yang Metal	丁 Yin Fire 巳 Snake
辛 Yin Metal	丙 Yang Fire 午 Horse
壬 Yang Water	己 Yin Earth 巳 Snake
癸 Yin Water	**戊 Yang Earth** **午 Horse**

The Direct Power on the Prosperity Pillars in bold can appear in the Hour Pillar.

The following examples illustrate each of the Direct Power on the Prosperity Pillars.

Example 2.27

Julio Iglesias, Spanish Singer-Songwriter,
September 23, 1943, 11:30 hours DST

Hour	Day	Month	Year
己	甲	辛	癸
Yin Earth	**Yang Wood**	**Yin Metal**	Yin Water
巳	申	酉	未
Snake	Monkey	**Rooster**	Sheep

Iglesias is a Yang Wood Day Stem. The Direct Power on the Prosperity Pillar Yin Metal Rooster is present in the Month. He is recognized as the most commercially successful Spanish singer in the world.

Example 2.28

Michelle Williams, American Actress,
September 9, 1980, 18:15 hours

Hour	Day	Month	Year
乙	乙	乙	庚
Yin Wood	**Yin Wood**	Yin Wood	**Yang Metal**
酉	酉	酉	申
Rooster	Rooster	Rooster	**Monkey**

Williams is a Yin Wood Day Stem. The Direct Power on the Prosperity Pillar Yang Metal Monkey is present in the Year. Note that it is also a Direct Power on the Nobleman Pillar. She has won two Golden Globe Awards and has been nominated for an Oscar four times.

Example 2.29

Lucy Liu, American Actress, December 2, 1968

Hour	Day	Month	Year
	丙	癸	戊
	Yang Fire	**Yin Water**	Yang Earth
	午	亥	申
	Horse	**Pig**	Monkey

Liu is a Yang Fire Day Stem. The Direct Power on the Prosperity Pillar Yin Water Pig is present in the Month. Note that it is also a Direct Power on the Nobleman Pillar. She has won two Screen Actors Guild Awards.

Example 2.30

Vanessa Paradis, French Singer and Actress, December 22, 1972, 05:20 hours

Hour	Day	Month	Year
癸	丁	壬	壬
Yin Water	**Yin Fire**	**Yang Water**	**Yang Water**
卯	亥	子	子
Rabbit	Pig	**Rat**	**Rat**

Paradis is a Yin Fire Day Stem. The Direct Power on the Prosperity Pillar Yang Water Rat is present in the Month and Year. Note that it is also a Direct Power as a Lunar Helper. She was awarded the Cesar Award for Most Promising Young Actress in 1991 (Yin Metal Sheep year).

Example 2.31

David Beckham, English Footballer,
May 2, 1975, 06:17 hours

Hour	Day	Month	Year
乙	戊	庚	乙
Yin Wood	**Yang Earth**	Yang Metal	**Yin Wood**
卯	申	辰	卯
Rabbit	Monkey	Dragon	**Rabbit**

Beckham is a Yang Earth Day Stem. The Direct Power on the Prosperity Pillar Yin Wood Rabbit is present in the Hour and Year. He is the first English player to win League titles in four countries: England, Spain, the United States and France.

Example 2.32

Herb Elliott, Australian Athlete,
February 25, 1938, 23:45 hours

Hour	Day	Month	Year
甲	己	甲	戊
Yang Wood	**Yin Earth**	**Yang Wood**	Yang Earth
子	丑	寅	寅
Rat	Ox	**Tiger**	Tiger

Elliot is a Yin Earth Day Stem. The Direct Power on the Prosperity Pillar Yang Wood Tiger is present in the Month. Note that there is also a Direct Power on the Nobleman Pillar Yang Wood Rat in the Hour. He won the 1500 metres in the Rome Olympics in record time in 1960 (Yang Metal Rat year).

Example 2.33

Robert Mitchum, American Actor,
August 6, 1917, 06:00 hours

Hour	Day	Month	Year
己	庚	丁	丁
Yin Earth	**Yang Metal**	Yin Fire	**Yin Fire**
卯	辰	未	巳
Rabbit	Dragon	Sheep	**Snake**

Mitchum is a Yang Metal Day Stem. The Direct Power on the Prosperity Pillar Yin Fire Snake is present in the Year. There is also a Direct Power on the Nobleman Pillar Yin Fire Sheep present in the Month. He received an Oscar nomination for Best Supporting Actor for *The Story of G.I. Joe* in 1945 (Yin Wood Rooster year).

Example 2.34

Pierre Cardin, Italian-French designer,
July 2, 1922, 14:00 hours

Hour	Day	Month	Year
乙	辛	丙	壬
Yin Wood	**Yin Metal**	**Yang Fire**	Yang Water
未	未	午	戌
Sheep	Sheep	**Horse**	Dog

Cardin is a Yin Metal Day Stem. The Direct Power on the Prosperity Pillar Yang Fire Horse is present in the Month. Note that it is also a Direct Power on the Nobleman Pillar. It is also a Direct Power as a Lunar Helper. Cardin is known for his avant-garde style and founded his fashion house in 1950 (Yang Metal Tiger year).

Example 2.35

Gladys Knight, American Singer and Actress, May 28, 1944, 19:52 hours DST

Hour	Day	Month	Year
己	壬	己	甲
Yin Earth	**Yang Water**	**Yin Earth**	Yang Wood
酉	辰	巳	申
Rooster	Dragon	**Snake**	Monkey

Knight is a Yang Water Day Master. The Direct Power on the Prosperity Pillar Yin Earth Snake is present in the Month. Note that it is also a Direct Power on the Nobleman Pillar. She has won seven Grammy Awards and had two US Number One hits.

Example 2.36

Johnny Depp, American Actor and Musician, June 9, 1963, 08:44 hours

Hour	Day	Month	Year
丙	癸	戊	癸
Yang Fire	**Yin Water**	**Yang Earth**	Yin Water
辰	未	午	卯
Dragon	Sheep	**Horse**	Rabbit

Depp is a Yin Water Day Stem. The Direct Power on the Prosperity Pillar Yang Earth Horse is present in the Month. He is one of the most commercially successful actors of all time from his starring role in the *Pirates of the Caribbean* movies.

Example 2.37

Martha Stewart, American Television Personality, August 3, 1941, 13:33 hours DST

Hour	Day	Month	Year
戊	癸	乙	辛
Yang Earth	**Yin Water**	Yin Wood	Yin Metal
午	未	未	巳
Horse	Sheep	Sheep	Snake

Stewart is a Yin Water Day Stem. The Direct Power on the Prosperity Pillar Yang Earth Horse is present in the Hour. Stewart has gained success in publishing, broadcasting and merchandising through her company *Martha Stewart Living Omnimedia*.

Wealth Producing Direct Power in the Branches

Within the Hidden Branches, there is a special configuration when Direct Power is produced by the Wealth, i.e. the element the Day Master controls, regardless of whether it is Direct (Opposite Polarity) or Indirect Wealth (Same Polarity).

This applies when the Day Stem is sitting on the hidden Wealth element that produces the hidden Direct Power element. Those who are born on such days have the potential to enjoy professional success.

Table 2.11 lists the Day Stem with the Direct Power and the Branch with hidden Wealth and Direct Power.

Table 2.11 Day Stem, Direct Power and the Branch with hidden Wealth and Direct Power

Day Stem	Direct Power	Branch With Hidden Wealth and Direct Power as per Day Stem
甲 Yang Wood	辛 Yin Metal	戌 Dog (戊 Yang Earth)
乙 Yin Wood	庚 Yang Metal	巳 Snake (戊 Yang Earth) 申 Monkey (戊 Yang Earth)
丙 Yang Fire	癸 Yin Water	丑 Ox (辛 Yin Metal)
丁 Yin Fire	壬 Yang Water	申 Monkey (庚 Yang Metal)
戊 Yang Earth	乙 Yin Wood	辰 Dragon (癸 Yin Water)
己 Yin Earth	甲 Yang Wood	亥 Pig (壬 Yang Water)
庚 Yang Metal	丁 Yin Fire	未 Sheep (乙 Yin Wood)
辛 Yin Metal	丙 Yang Fire	寅 Tiger (甲 Yang Wood)
壬 Yang Water	己 Yin Earth	午 Horse (丁 Yin Fire) 未 Sheep (丁 Yin Fire)
癸 Yin Water	戊 Yang Earth	巳 Snake (丙 Yang Fire)

For example, for a Yang Wood Day Stem, the Direct Power is Yin Metal. This is hidden in the Dog. There is also Yang Earth hidden in the Dog, which represents the Wealth element for Yang Wood. Within the Dog, Yang Earth representing Wealth produces the Direct Power Yin Metal.

For a Yin Water Day Stem, the Direct Power is Yang Earth. This is hidden in the Snake. There is also Yang Fire hidden in the Snake, which represents the Wealth element for Yin Water. Within the Snake, Yang Fire representing Wealth produces the Direct Power Yang Earth.

Table 2.12 lists the six days that are Sitting on a Branch with Wealth element producing Direct Power.

Table 2.12 Six Days Sitting on a Branch with Wealth producing Direct Power

甲 Yang Wood	乙 Yin Wood	戊 Yang Earth	己 Yin Earth	壬 Yang Water	癸 Yin Water
戌 Dog	巳 Snake	辰 Dragon	亥 Pig	午 Horse	巳 Snake

Those who are born on such days have the potential to enjoy professional success.

The following examples consider these days.

Example 2.38

Francis Ford Coppola, American Film Director, April 7, 1939, 01:38 hours

Hour	Day	Month	Year
乙	甲	丁	己
Yin Wood	**Yang Wood**	Yin Fire	Yin Earth
丑	戌	卯	卯
Ox	**Dog**	Rabbit	Rabbit

Coppola is born on a Yang Wood Dog day, which is sitting on both the Wealth and Direct Power. He has received five Oscars for his work.

Example 2.39

Rihanna, Barbadian Singer and Actress,
February 20, 1988, 08:50 hours

Hour	Day	Month	Year
庚	乙	甲	戊
Yang Metal	**Yin Wood**	Yang Wood	Yang Earth
辰	巳	寅	辰
Dragon	**Snake**	Tiger	Dragon

Rihanna is born on a Yin Wood Snake day, which is sitting on both the Wealth and Direct Power. She has scored 14 US Number One hits and sold more than 250 million records worldwide.

Example 2.40

Abdullah II of Jordan, Jordanian Royalty,
January 30, 1962, 05:23 hours

Hour	Day	Month	Year
乙	戊	辛	辛
Yin Wood	**Yang Earth**	Yin Metal	Yin Metal
卯	辰	丑	丑
Rabbit	**Dragon**	Ox	Ox

King Abdullah is born on a Yang Earth Dragon day, which sits on both the Wealth and Direct Power. He has ruled Jordan since 1999 (Yin Earth Rabbit year).

Example 2.41

Jon Bon Jovi, American Singer and Actor *Bon Jovi*,
March 2, 1962, 20:45 hours

Hour	Day	Month	Year
甲	己	壬	壬
Yang Wood	**Yin Earth**	Yang Water	Yang Water
戌	亥	寅	寅
Dog	**Pig**	Tiger	Tiger

Bon Jovi is born on a Yin Earth Pig day, which sits on the Wealth and Direct Power. He is the lead singer of *Bon Jovi*, which has sold more than 130 million records, making them one of the best-selling American rock bands.

Example 2.42

Jane Fonda, American Actress,
December 21, 1937, 09:14 hours

Hour	Day	Month	Year
乙	壬	壬	丁
Yin Wood	**Yang Water**	Yang Water	Yin Fire
巳	午	子	丑
Snake	**Horse**	Rat	Ox

Fonda is born on a Yang Water Horse day, which sits on the Wealth and Direct Power. Recognized as a film icon, she has won two Oscars for Best Actress. Her workout video became the top-selling VHS of the 20th century in 1982 (Yang Water Dog year).

Example 2.43

Jackie Chan, Hong Kong Actor and Martial Artist, April 7, 1954, 09:45 hours

Hour	Day	Month	Year
丁	癸	戊	甲
Yin Fire	Yin Water	Yang Earth	Yang Wood
巳	巳	辰	午
Snake	Snake	Dragon	Horse

Chan is born on a Yin Water Snake day, which sits on the Wealth and Direct Power. He has appeared in more than 150 films and is one of the most popular action film stars of all time.

Summary

In summary, what to look for in a chart with regard to the Direct Power:

1. Direct Power Sitting on the Nobleman Star.
2. Direct Power as a Solar or Lunar Helper.
3. Direct Power Sitting on the Academic Star.
4. Direct Power Sitting on the Prosperity Pillar.
5. Days Sitting on the Wealth and Direct Power.

Chapter Three

Chapter Three Seven Killings

The Power element that is of the same polarity of the Day Stem is known as the Seven Killings or Indirect Power. Direct Power is the Power element that is of the opposite polarity of the Day Stem. For example, a Yang Fire Day Master has Water as its Power element. The Power element that is of the opposite polarity is Yin Water. This is Direct Power. The Power element that is of the same polarity is Yang Water. This is the Seven Killings.

Table 3.1 lists the Day Stem with the Seven Killings.

Table 3.1 Day Stem and Seven Killings

Day Stem	Seven Killings
甲 Yang Wood	庚 Yang Metal
乙 Yin Wood	辛 Yin Metal
丙 Yang Fire	壬 Yang Water
丁 Yin Fire	癸 Yin Water
戊 Yang Earth	甲 Yang Wood
己 Yin Earth	乙 Yin Wood
庚 Yang Metal	丙 Yang Fire
辛 Yin Metal	丁 Yin Fire
壬 Yang Water	戊 Yang Earth
癸 Yin Water	己 Yin Earth

While the Direct Power indicates position, the Seven Killings indicates power. There is also significant pressure if the person does not have the ability to match their ambition. The Seven Killings brings forth fame, unlike the Direct Power Stem.

Seven Killings Sitting on Earth Branch in the Year Pillar

When the Seven Killings is Sitting on the Earth Branch in the Year Pillar, it indicates a person born into modest circumstances who was able to improve their social and economic status.

Table 3.2 indicates the Day Stem and the Seven Killings Sitting on the Earth Branch in the Year Pillar.

Table 3.2 Day Stem and Seven Killings Sitting on the Earth Branch in the Year Pillar

Day Stem	Seven Killings Sitting on the Earth Branch	Seven Killings Sitting on the Earth Branch
甲 Yang Wood	庚 Yang Metal 辰 Dragon	庚 Yang Metal 戌 Dog
乙 Yin Wood	辛 Yin Metal 丑 Ox	辛 Yin Metal 未 Sheep
丙 Yang Fire	壬 Yang Water 辰 Dragon	壬 Yang Water 戌 Dog
丁 Yin Fire	癸 Yin Water 丑 Ox	癸 Yin Water 未 Sheep
戊 Yang Earth	甲 Yang Wood 辰 Dragon	甲 Yang Wood 戌 Dog
己 Yin Earth	乙 Yin Wood 丑 Ox	乙 Yin Wood 未 Sheep
庚 Yang Metal	丙 Yang Fire 辰 Dragon	丙 Yang Fire 戌 Dog
辛 Yin Metal	丁 Yin Fire 丑 Ox	丁 Yin Fire 未 Sheep
壬 Yang Water	戊 Yang Earth 辰 Dragon	戊 Yang Earth 戌 Dog
癸 Yin Water	己 Yin Earth 丑 Ox	己 Yin Earth 未 Sheep

The following 20 examples illustrate each Seven Killings Sitting on the Earth Branch in the Year Pillar.

Example 3.1

Al Jarreau, American Singer and Musician, March 12, 1940, 01:20 hours

Hour	Day	Month	Year
乙	甲	己	庚
Yin Wood	**Yang Wood**	Yin Earth	**Yang Metal**
丑	寅	卯	辰
Ox	Tiger	Rabbit	**Dragon**

Jarreau is a Yang Wood Day Stem. The Seven Killings Yang Metal is present in the Year Pillar and Sitting on the Dragon Earth Branch. Born in Milwaukee, Wisconsin, Jarreau was the fifth of six children. His father was a minister and singer, while his mother was a church pianist.

Example 3.2

Taraji P. Henson, American Actress, September 11, 1970, 04:00 hours

Hour	Day	Month	Year
丙	甲	乙	庚
Yang Fire	**Yang Wood**	Yin Wood	**Yang Metal**
寅	午	酉	戌
Tiger	Horse	Rooster	**Dog**

Henson is a Yang Wood Day Stem. The Seven Killings Yang Metal is present in the Year Pillar and Sitting on the Dog Earth Branch. Henson was born in Washington D.C. Her father was a janitor and metal worker, while her mother was a corporate manager at a department store.

Example 3.3

Gary Cooper, American Actor,
May 7, 1901, 05:45 hours

Hour	Day	Month	Year
己	乙	壬	辛
Yin Earth	**Yin Wood**	Yang Water	**Yin Metal**
卯	酉	辰	丑
Rabbit	Rooster	Dragon	**Ox**

Cooper is a Yin Wood Day Stem. The Seven Killings Yin Metal is present in the Year Pillar and Sitting on the Ox Earth Branch. Cooper was born in Helena, Montana, and his father was a lawyer, rancher and Montana Supreme Court justice.

Example 3.4

Anne Bancroft, American Actress,
September 17, 1931, 11:50 hours DST

Hour	Day	Month	Year
辛	乙	丁	辛
Yin Metal	**Yin Wood**	Yin Fire	**Yin Metal**
巳	亥	酉	未
Snake	Pig	Rooster	**Sheep**

Bancroft is a Yin Wood Day Stem. The Seven Killings Yin Metal is present in the Year Pillar and Sitting on the Sheep Earth Branch. The middle of three daughters, Bancroft was born in the Bronx, New York City to Italian immigrants. Her father was a dress pattern maker and her mother a telephone operator.

Example 3.5

Steven Seagal, American Actor and Martial Artist, April 10, 1952, 13:54 hours

Hour	Day	Month	Year
乙	丙	甲	壬
Yin Wood	**Yang Fire**	Yang Wood	**Yang Water**
未	戌	辰	辰
Sheep	Dog	Dragon	**Dragon**

Seagal is a Yang Fire Day Stem. The Seven Killings Yang Water is present in the Year Pillar and Sitting on the Dragon Earth Branch. Seagal was born in Lansing, Michigan. His father was a high school mathematics teacher and his mother a medical technician.

Example 3.6

Ava Gardner, American Actress, December 24, 1922, 19:10 hours

Hour	Day	Month	Year
戊	丙	壬	壬
Yang Earth	**Yang Fire**	Yang Water	**Yang Water**
戌	寅	子	戌
Dog	Tiger	Rat	**Dog**

Gardner is a Yang Fire Day Stem. The Seven Killings Yang Water is present in the Year Pillar and Sitting on the Dog Earth Branch. The youngest of seven children, Gardner was born in North Carolina. Her parents were tobacco sharecroppers.

Example 3.7

Kate Moss, English Model and Businesswoman,
January 16, 1974, 17:00 hours

Hour	Day	Month	**Year**
己	丁	乙	**癸**
Yin Earth	**Yin Fire**	Yin Wood	**Yin Water**
酉	巳	丑	**丑**
Rooster	Snake	Ox	**Ox**

Moss is a Yin Fire Day Stem. The Seven Killings Yin Water is present in the Year Pillar and Sitting on an Ox Earth Branch. Moss was born in Croydon, London. Her father was an airline employee and her mother a barmaid.

Example 3.8

Sam Shepard, American Actor and Playwright,
November 5, 1943, 15:45 hours

Hour	Day	Month	**Year**
戊	丁	癸	**癸**
Yang Earth	**Yin Fire**	Yin Water	**Yin Water**
申	卯	亥	**未**
Monkey	Rabbit	Pig	**Sheep**

Shepard is a Yin Fire Day Stem. The Seven Killings Yin Water is present in the Year Pillar and Sitting on a Sheep Earth Branch. Shepard was born in the Chicago suburb of Fort Sheridan. His father was a teacher and farmer, while his mother was a teacher.

Example 3.9

Wendy Williams, American Television Host,
July 18, 1964, 21:30 hours DST

Hour	Day	Month	Year
壬	戊	辛	甲
Yang Water	**Yang Earth**	Yin Metal	**Yang Wood**
戌	辰	未	辰
Dog	Dragon	Sheep	**Dragon**

Williams is a Yang Earth Day Stem. The Seven Killings Yang Wood is present in the Year Pillar and Sitting on a Dragon Earth Branch. Williams was born in New Jersey, the second of three children. Her father was a teacher and school principal and her mother a special education teacher.

Example 3.10

Charley Pride, American Singer and Baseball Player,
March 18, 1934, 08:00 hours

Hour	Day	Month	Year
丙	戊	丁	甲
Yang Fire	**Yang Earth**	Yin Fire	**Yang Wood**
辰	子	卯	戌
Dragon	Rat	Rabbit	**Dog**

Pride is a Yang Earth Day Stem. The Seven Killings Yang Wood is present in the Year Pillar and Sitting on a Dog Earth Branch. Pride was born in Mississippi, the fourth of eleven children. His parents were sharecroppers.

Example 3.11

Jeanne Crain, American Actress, May 25, 1925, 17:00 hours

Hour	Day	Month	Year
癸	己	辛	乙
Yin Water	**Yin Earth**	Yin Metal	**Yin Wood**
酉	酉	巳	丑
Rooster	Rooster	Snake	**Ox**

Crain is a Yin Earth Day Stem. The Seven Killings Yin Wood is present in the Year Pillar and Sitting on an Ox Earth Branch. Crain was born in Bairstow, California. Her father was a school teacher.

Example 3.12

Zucchero, Italian Singer and Musician, September 25, 1955, 18:15 hours

Hour	Day	Month	Year
癸	己	乙	乙
Yin Water	**Yin Earth**	Yin Wood	**Yin Wood**
酉	丑	酉	未
Rooster	Ox	Rooster	**Sheep**

Zucchero is a Yin Earth Day Stem. The Seven Killings Yin Wood is present in the Year Pillar and Sitting on a Sheep Earth Branch. Zucchero was born in a small village near Reggio Emilia. Both his parents came from rural families.

Example 3.13

Kirk Douglas, American Actor,
December 9, 1916, 10:15 hours

Hour	Day	Month	Year
辛	**庚**	庚	**丙**
Yin Metal	**Yang Metal**	Yang Metal	**Yang Fire**
巳	辰	子	辰
Snake	Dragon	Rat	**Dragon**

Douglas is a Yang Metal Day Stem. The Seven Killings Yang Fire is present in the Year Pillar and Sitting on a Dragon Earth Branch. Douglas was born in New York, the fourth of seven children and the only son. His parents were immigrants from present-day Belarus and his father was a ragman.

Example 3.14

Gianni Versace, Italian Fashion Designer,
December 2, 1946, 06:00 hours

Hour	Day	Month	Year
己	**庚**	庚	**丙**
Yin Earth	**Yang Metal**	Yang Metal	**Yang Fire**
卯	戌	子	戌
Rabbit	Dog	Rat	**Dog**

Versace is a Yang Metal Day Stem. The Seven Killings Yang Fire is present in the Year Pillar and Sitting on a Dog Earth Branch. Versace was born in Reggio Calabria. His mother was a dressmaker.

Example 3.15

Sir Ridley Scott, English Filmmaker, November 30, 1937

Hour	Day	Month	Year
	辛	辛	丁
	Yin Metal	Yin Metal	**Yin Fire**
	酉	亥	丑
	Rooster	Pig	**Ox**

Scott is a Yin Metal Day Stem. The Seven Killings Yin Fire is present in the Year Pillar and Sitting on an Ox Earth Branch. Born in South Shields, County Durham, Scott is one of three sons. His father was in the army.

Example 3.16

Sir Laurence Olivier, English Actor and Director, May 22, 1907, 05:00 hours

Hour	Day	Month	Year
辛	辛	乙	丁
Yin Metal	**Yin Metal**	Yin Wood	**Yin Fire**
卯	未	巳	未
Rabbit	Sheep	Snake	**Sheep**

Olivier is a Yin Metal Day Stem. The Seven Killings Yin Fire is present in the Year Pillar and Sitting over a Sheep Earth Branch. Born in Surrey, Olivier was the youngest of three children. His father was a reverend.

Example 3.17

Serge Gainsbourg, French Singer and Actor,
April 2, 1928, 04:55 hours

Hour	Day	Month	Year
壬	壬	乙	戊
Yang Water	**Yang Water**	Yin Wood	**Yang Earth**
寅	申	卯	辰
Tiger	Monkey	Rabbit	**Dragon**

Gainsbourg is a Yang Water Day Stem. The Seven Killings Yang Earth is present in the Year Pillar and Sitting on a Dragon Earth Branch. Gainsbourg was born in Paris to Ukrainian-Jewish immigrants. His father was a pianist in cabarets and casinos.

Example 3.18

Andrea Bocelli, Italian Singer-Songwriter,
September 22, 1958, 05:15 hours

Hour	Day	Month	Year
癸	壬	辛	戊
Yin Water	**Yang Water**	Yin Metal	**Yang Earth**
卯	寅	酉	戌
Rabbit	Tiger	Rooster	**Dog**

Bocelli is a Yang Water Day Stem. The Seven Killings Yang Earth is present in the Year Pillar and Sitting on a Dog Earth Branch. Bocelli was born in a small village in Tuscany and grew up on a farm where his parents sold machinery and made wine.

Example 3.19

Richard Gere, American Actor,
August 31, 1949, 02:00 hours

Hour	Day	Month	Year
癸	癸	壬	己
Yin Water	**Yin Water**	Yang Water	**Yin Earth**
丑	巳	申	丑
Ox	Snake	Monkey	**Ox**

Gere is a Yin Water Day Stem. The Seven Killings Yin Earth is present in the Year Pillar and Sitting on an Ox Earth Branch. Gere was born in Philadelphia. His father was an insurance agent.

Example 3.20

Shane Filan, Irish Singer *Westlife*, July 5, 1979, 08:45 hours

Hour	Day	Month	Year
丙	癸	辛	己
Yang Fire	**Yin Water**	Yin Metal	**Yin Earth**
辰	酉	未	未
Dragon	Rooster	Sheep	**Sheep**

Filan is a Yin Water Day Stem. The Seven Killings Yin Earth is present in the Year Pillar and Sitting on a Sheep Earth Branch. Filan was born in Sligo, Ireland, the youngest of seven siblings. His parents ran a diner.

Seven Killings Sitting on the Earth Branch in the Hour Pillar

When the Seven Killings sits on the Earth Branch in the Hour Pillar, the person will receive much blessing and good fortune.

With regard to having the Seven Killings Sitting on the Earth Branch in the Hour Pillar, there are only four possibilities, which are listed in Table 3.3.

Table 3.3 Day Stem and Seven Killings Sitting on the Earth Branch in the Hour Pillar

Day Stem	Seven Killings Sitting on the Earth Branch in Hour Pillar
丙 Yang Fire	壬 Yang Water 辰 Dragon
己 Yin Earth	乙 Yin Wood 丑 Ox
庚 Yang Metal	丙 Yang Fire 戌 Dog
癸 Yin Water	己 Yin Earth 未 Sheep

The following eight examples illustrate each Seven Killings Sitting on the Earth Branch in the Hour Pillar.

Example 3.21

Steve Carell, American Actor and Comedian, August 16, 1962, 08:59 hours

Hour	Day	Month	Year
壬	丙	戊	壬
Yang Water	**Yang Fire**	Yang Earth	Yang Water
辰	戌	申	寅
Dragon	Dog	Monkey	Tiger

Carrell is a Yang Fire Day Stem. The Seven Killings Yang Water is Sitting on a Dragon Earth Branch in the Hour Pillar. Carell has been recognized as "America's Funniest Man" by *Life* magazine.

Example 3.22

Jordin Sparks, American Singer-Songwriter and Actress, December 22, 1989, 08:45 hours

Hour	Day	Month	Year
壬	丙	丙	己
Yang Water	**Yang Fire**	Yang Fire	Yin Earth
辰	辰	子	巳
Dragon	Dragon	Rat	Snake

Sparks is a Yang Fire Day Stem. The Seven Killings Yang Water is Sitting on a Dragon Branch in the Hour Pillar. In 2007 (Yin Fire Pig year), Sparks rose to fame when she won the sixth season of *American Idol*.

Example 3.23

Isabelle Adjani, French Actress,
June 27, 1955, 01:00 hours

Hour	Day	Month	Year
乙	己	壬	乙
Yin Wood	**Yin Earth**	Yang Water	**Yin Wood**
丑	未	午	未
Ox	Sheep	Horse	**Sheep**

Adjani is a Yin Earth Day Stem. The Seven Killings Yin Wood is Sitting on an Ox Earth Branch in the Hour Pillar. She is the only person to win five Cesar Awards. The Seven Killings Yin Wood is also present in the Year Pillar and Sitting on a Sheep Earth Branch. Adjani was born in Paris to an Algerian father and a German mother.

Example 3.24

Morgan Freeman, American Actor,
June 1, 1937, 02:00 hours

Hour	Day	Month	Year
乙	己	乙	丁
Yin Wood	**Yin Earth**	Yin Wood	Yin Fire
丑	未	巳	丑
Ox	Sheep	Snake	Ox

Freeman is a Yin Earth Day Stem. The Seven Killings Yin Wood is Sitting on an Ox Earth Branch in the Hour Pillar. Freeman has enjoyed a five-decade career and has received an Oscar for Best Supporting Actor.

Example 3.25

Andrew Garfield, British and American Actor,
August 20, 1983, 20:40 hours

Hour	Day	Month	Year
丙	庚	庚	癸
Yang Fire	**Yang Metal**	Yang Metal	Yin Water
戌	辰	申	亥
Dog	Dragon	Monkey	Pig

Garfield is a Yang Metal Day Stem. The Seven Killings Yang Fire is Sitting on a Dog Earth Branch in the Hour Pillar. In 2012 (Yang Water Dragon year), he gained recognition for playing Spider-Man.

Example 3.26

Kim Wilde, English Singer and Television Presenter,
November 18, 1960, 20:00 hours

Hour	Day	Month	Year
丙	庚	丙	庚
Yang Fire	**Yang Metal**	Yang Fire	Yang Metal
戌	戌	戌	子
Dog	Dog	Dog	Rat

Wilde is a Yang Metal Day Stem. The Seven Killings Yang Fire is Sitting on a Dog Earth Branch in the Hour Pillar. Note that the Yang Fire Dog Month Pillar is not relevant. Wilde is the most-charted British female solo act of the 1980s and has branched into landscape gardening.

Example 3.27

Mother Teresa, Albanian-Indian Nun and Missionary, August 26, 1910, 14:25 hours

Hour	Day	Month	Year
己	癸	甲	庚
Yin Earth	**Yin Water**	Yang Wood	Yang Metal
未	亥	申	戌
Sheep	Pig	Monkey	Dog

Mother Teresa is a Yin Water Day Stem. The Seven Killings Yin Earth is Sitting on a Sheep Earth Branch in the Hour Pillar. Mother Teresa was canonised in the Catholic Church as Saint Teresa of Calcutta in 2016 (Yang Fire Monkey year).

Example 3.28

Gaspard Ulliel, French Actor and Model, November 25, 1984, 14:50 hours

Hour	Day	Month	Year
己	癸	乙	甲
Yin Earth	**Yin Water**	Yin Wood	Yang Wood
未	亥	亥	子
Sheep	Pig	Pig	Rat

Ulliel is a Yin Water Day Stem. The Seven Killings Yin Earth is Sitting on a Sheep Earth Branch in the Hour Pillar. Ulliel became a *Knight of the Order of Arts and Letters* in France in 2015 (Yin Wood Sheep year).

Seven Killings in the Hour Pillar

When the Seven Killings is present in the Hour Pillar, the person will have a good reputation. The Seven Killings can be present in the Hour Stem, Hour Branch or in both the Hour Stem and Hour Branch.

Table 3.4 lists the Day Stem with the corresponding Hour Pillar that contains the Seven Killings.

Table 3.4 Day Stem and Hour Pillar with Seven Killings

Day Stem	Seven Killings in the Hour Pillar
甲 Yang Wood	己 Yin Earth 庚 Yang Metal 壬 Yang Water 巳 Snake　　午 Horse　　申 Monkey
乙 Yin Wood	丁 Yin Fire 辛 Yin Metal 乙 Yin Wood 丙 Yang Fire 丑 Ox　　巳 Snake　　酉 Rooster　　戌 Dog
丙 Yang Fire	壬 Yang Water 丙 Yang Fire 己 Yin Earth 辰 Dragon　　申 Monkey　亥 Pig
丁 Yin Fire	庚 Yang Metal 辛 Yin Metal 癸 Yin Water 甲 Yang Wood 子 Rat　　丑 Ox　　卯 Rabbit　　辰 Dragon
戊 Yang Earth	**甲 Yang Wood** 癸 Yin Water **寅 Tiger**　　亥 Pig
己 Yin Earth	**乙 Yin Wood** 丁 Yin Fire 戊 Yang Earth 辛 Yin Metal 乙 Yin Wood **丑 Ox**　　卯 Rabbit 辰 Dragon 未 Sheep　亥 Pig
庚 Yang Metal	丙 Yang Fire 戊 Yang Earth 辛 Yin Metal 丙 Yang Fire 子 Rat　　寅 Tiger　　巳 Snake　　戌 Dog

辛 Yin Metal	甲 Yang Wood 乙 Yin Wood 丁 Yin Fire 戊 Yang Earth 午 Horse　　未 Sheep　　酉 Rooster 戌 Dog
壬 Yang Water	壬 Yang Water 甲 Yang Wood 乙 Yin Wood **戊 Yang Earth** 寅 Tiger　　辰 Dragon　　巳 Snake　　**申 Monkey** 庚 Yang Metal 戌 Dog
癸 Yin Water	癸 Yin Water 戊 Yang Earth 己 **Yin Earth** 丑 Ox　　　午 Horse　　　**未 Sheep**

The Pillars that are in bold indicate the Seven Killings present in both the Stem and the Branch.

The following examples illustrate all the Pillars with Seven Killings present in the Hour. When the Seven Killings is hidden in the Branch, it is indicated.

Example 3.29

Harry Belafonte, Jamaican-American Singer and Actor, March 1, 1927, 10:30 hours

Hour	Day	Month	Year
己	甲	壬	丁
Yin Earth	**Yang Wood**	Yang Water	Yin Fire
巳	午	寅	卯
Snake	Horse	Tiger	Rabbit

庚 Yang Metal

Belafonte is a Yang Wood Day Stem. The Seven Killings Yang Metal is hidden in the Snake Hour Branch. In 2022 (Yang Water Tiger year), he became the oldest living person to be inducted into the Rock and Roll Hall of Fame.

Example 3.30

Jerry Lewis, American Actor and Comedian,
March 16, 1926, 12:15 hours

Hour	Day	Month	Year
庚	甲	辛	丙
Yang Metal	**Yang Wood**	Yin Metal	Yang Fire
午	辰	卯	寅
Horse	Dragon	Rabbit	Tiger

Lewis is a Yang Wood Day Stem. The Seven Killings Yang Metal is present in the Hour Stem. Over an eight decade career, he became known as the King of Comedy. Lewis was also the chairman of the Muscular Dystrophy Association. He hosted The Jerry Lewis Telethon over the Labor Day weekend for 44 years.

Example 3.31

Barbara Mandrell, American Country Singer,
December 25, 1948, 15:42 hours

Hour	Day	Month	Year
壬	甲	甲	戊
Yang Water	**Yang Wood**	Yang Wood	Yang Earth
申	申	子	子
Monkey	Monkey	Rat	Rat
庚 **Yang Metal**			

Mandrell is a Yang Wood Day Stem. The Seven Killings Yang Metal is hidden in the Monkey Hour Branch. She had six Number One Singles on the country music charts. In 2009 (Yin Earth Ox year), Mandrell was inducted into the Country Music Hall of Fame.

Example 3.32

Sir Mick Jagger, English Singer and Actor *Rolling Stones*, July 26, 1943, 02:30 hours

Hour	Day	Month	Year
丁	乙	己	癸
Yin Fire	**Yin Wood**	Yin Earth	Yin Water
丑	酉	未	未
Ox	Rooster	Sheep	Sheep
辛 **Yin Metal**			

Jagger is a Yin Wood Day Stem. The Seven Killings Yin Metal is hidden in the Ox Hour Branch. He has scored 13 UK and US Number One Singles. In 2003 (Yin Water Sheep year), Jagger was knighted for his services to popular music.

Example 3.33

Kenny Rogers, American Singer and Actor, August 21, 1938, 11:29 hours DST

Hour	Day	Month	Year
辛	乙	庚	戊
Yin Metal	**Yin Wood**	Yang Metal	Yang Earth
巳	酉	申	寅
Snake	Rooster	Monkey	Tiger

Rogers is a Yin Wood Day Stem. The Seven Killings Yin Metal is present in the Hour Stem. He sold more than 100 million records worldwide during his lifetime. In 2013 (Yin Water Snake year), Rogers was inducted into the Country Music Hall of Fame.

Example 3.34

Betty White, American Actress and Comedian, January 17, 1922, 18:38 hours

Hour	Day	Month	Year
乙	乙	辛	辛
Yin Wood	**Yin Wood**	Yin Metal	Yin Metal
酉	酉	丑	酉
Rooster	Rooster	Ox	Rooster
辛 **Yin Metal**			

White is a Yin Wood Day Stem. The Seven Killings Yin Metal is hidden in the Rooster Hour Branch. In 2014 (Yang Wood Horse year), she earned a Guinness World Record for Longest TV career by an entertainer (female).

Example 3.35

Dame Joanna Lumley, English Actress and Comedian, May 1, 1946, 19:30 hours

Hour	Day	Month	Year
丙	乙	癸	丙
Yang Fire	**Yin Wood**	Yin Water	Yang Fire
戌	亥	巳	戌
Dog	Pig	Snake	Dog
辛 **Yin Metal**			

Lumley is a Yin Wood Day Stem. The Seven Killings Yin Metal is hidden in the Dog Hour Branch. In 2022 (Yang Water Tiger year), she was made a Dame of the British Empire for services to drama, entertainment and charity.

Example 3.36

Gerard Depardieu, French Actor,
December 27, 1948, 08:00 hours

Hour	Day	Month	Year
壬	丙	甲	戊
Yang Water	**Yang Fire**	Yang Wood	Yang Earth
辰	戌	子	子
Dragon	Dog	Rat	Rat

Depardieu is a Yang Fire Day Stem. The Seven Killings Yang Water is present in the Hour Stem. He is the second highest grossing actor in the history of French cinema. Depardieu has appeared in more than 250 films as a lead.

Example 3.37

Baron Andrew Lloyd Webber, English Composer and
Musical Theatre Impresario, March 22, 1948, 16:00 hours

Hour	Day	Month	Year
丙	丙	乙	戊
Yang Fire	**Yang Fire**	Yin Wood	Yang Earth
申	午	卯	子
Monkey	Horse	Rabbit	Rat
壬 **Yang Water**			

Webber is a Yang Fire Day Stem. The Seven Killings Yang Water is hidden in the Monkey Hour Branch. He has been awarded both a knighthood and peerage for his contribution to the arts. In 2001 (Yin Metal Snake year), the *New York Times* referred to him as the most commercially successful composer in history.

Example 3.38

Mae West, American Actress and Singer, August 17, 1893, 22:30 hours

Hour	Day	Month	Year
己	丙	庚	癸
Yin Earth	**Yang Fire**	Yang Metal	Yin Water
亥	戌	申	巳
Pig	Dog	Monkey	Snake

壬 **Yang Water**

West is a Yang Fire Day Stem. The Seven Killings Yang Water is hidden in the Pig Hour Branch. She enjoyed a seven decade career. West was posthumously voted as the 15th greatest female screen legend of American cinema.

Example 3.39

Garry Kasparov, Russian Chess Grandmaster, April 13, 1963, 23:45 hours

Hour	Day	Month	Year
庚	丁	丙	癸
Yang Metal	**Yin Fire**	Yang Fire	Yin Water
子	亥	辰	卯
Rat	Pig	Dragon	Rabbit

癸 **Yin Water**

Kasparov is a Yin Fire Day Stem. The Seven Killings Yin Water is hidden in the Rat Hour Branch. He was ranked World Number One in chess for a record 255 months. In 1985 (Yin Wood Ox year), Kasparov became the youngest ever World Chess Champion.

Example 3.40

Jeremy Irons, English Actor,
September 19, 1948, 02:00 hours

Hour	Day	Month	Year
辛	丁	辛	戊
Yin Metal	**Yin Fire**	Yin Metal	Yang Earth
丑	未	酉	子
Ox	Sheep	Rooster	Rat
癸 **Yin Water**			

Irons is a Yin Fire Day Stem. The Seven Killings Yin Water is hidden in the Ox Hour Branch. He is one of the few actors who has achieved the Triple Crown of Acting, winning an Oscar for film, an Emmy for television and a Tony for theatre.

Example 3.41

Taylor Swift, American Singer-Songwriter,
December 13, 1989, 05:17 hours

Hour	Day	Month	Year
癸	丁	丙	己
Yin Water	**Yin Fire**	Yang Fire	Yin Earth
卯	未	子	巳
Rabbit	Sheep	Rat	Snake

Swift is a Yin Fire Day Stem. The Seven Killings Yin Water is present in the Hour Stem. She has sold more than 200 million records worldwide, making her one of the best selling musicians of all time.

Example 3.42

Diane Warren, American Songwriter,
September 7, 1956, 08:24 hours

Hour	Day	Month	Year
甲	丁	丁	丙
Yang Wood	**Yin Fire**	Yin Fire	Yang Fire
辰	丑	酉	申
Dragon	Ox	Rooster	Monkey
癸 **Yin Water**			

Warren is a Yin Fire Day Stem. The Seven Killings Yin Water is hidden in the Dragon Hour Branch. She has written nine US Number One Singles. Warren has also been inducted into the Songwriters Hall of Fame.

Example 3.43

Philippe Starck, French Architect and Designer,
January 18, 1949, 04:40 hours

Hour	Day	Month	Year
甲	戊	乙	戊
Yang Wood	**Yang Earth**	Yin Wood	Yang Earth
寅	申	丑	子
Tiger	Monkey	Ox	Rat
甲 **Yang Wood**			

Starck is a Yang Earth Day Stem. The Seven Killings Yang Wood is present in the Hour Stem and also hidden in the Tiger Hour Branch. He is known for his wide range of designs, including architecture, interior design, household objects and furniture.

Example 3.44

Montserrat Caballe, Spanish Soprano,
April 12, 1933, 21:00 hours

Hour	Day	Month	Year
癸	戊	丙	癸
Yin Water	**Yang Earth**	Yang Fire	Yin Water
亥	申	辰	酉
Pig	Monkey	Dragon	Rooster

甲 Yang Wood

Caballe is a Yang Earth Day Stem. The Seven Killings Yang Wood is hidden in the Pig Hour Branch. In 1966 (Yang Fire Horse year), she was awarded a Dame Commander of the Order of Isabella the Catholic. In 2005 (Yin Wood Rooster year), Caballe was awarded a Legion of Honour.

Example 3.45

Audrey Hepburn, British Actress and Humanitarian,
May 4, 1929, 03:00 hours DST

Hour	Day	Month	Year
乙	己	戊	己
Yin Wood	Yin Earth	Yang Earth	Yin Earth
丑	酉	辰	巳
Ox	Rooster	Dragon	Snake

Hepburn is a Yin Earth Day Stem. The Seven Killings Yin Wood is present in the Hour Stem. She is recognized as both a film and fashion icon. In 1992 (Yang Water Monkey year), Hepburn received the US Presidential Medal of Freedom in recognition of her work as a UNICEF Goodwill Ambassador.

Example 3.46

George Michael, English Singer-Songwriter,
June 25, 1963, 06:00 hours

Hour	Day	Month	Year
丁	己	戊	癸
Yin Fire	**Yin Earth**	Yang Earth	Yin Water
卯	亥	午	卯
Rabbit	Pig	Horse	Rabbit
乙 **Yin Wood**			

Michael is a Yin Earth Day Stem. The Seven Killings Yin Wood is hidden in the Rabbit Hour Branch. He scored eight US Number One Singles and sold more than 120 million records worldwide.

Example 3.47

Bjork, Icelandic Singer and Actress,
November 21, 1965, 07:50 hours

Hour	Day	Month	Year
戊	己	丁	乙
Yang Earth	**Yin Earth**	Yin Fire	Yin Wood
辰	卯	亥	巳
Dragon	Rabbit	Pig	Snake
乙 **Yin Wood**			

Bjork is a Yin Earth Day Stem. The Seven Killings Yin Wood is hidden in the Dragon Hour Branch. She has a four-decade career in music and sold between 20 and 40 million records worldwide.

Example 3.48

Luc Besson, French Film Director,
March 18, 1959, 13:45 hours

Hour	Day	Month	Year
辛	己	丁	己
Yin Metal	**Yin Earth**	Yin Fire	Yin Earth
未	亥	卯	亥
Sheep	Pig	Rabbit	Pig
乙 **Yin Wood**			

Besson is a Yin Earth Day Stem. The Seven Killings Yin Wood is hidden in the Sheep Hour Branch. He has been involved in the creation of more than 50 films. In 1997 (Yin Fire Ox year), he won a Cesar Award for Best Director for *The Fifth Element*.

Example 3.49

Diana Ross, American Singer and Actress,
March 26, 1944, 23:46 hours DST

Day	Day	Month	Year
乙	己	戊	甲
Yin Wood	**Yin Earth**	Yang Earth	Yang Wood
亥	丑	辰	申
Pig	Ox	Dragon	Monkey

Ross is a Yin Earth Day Stem. The Seven Killings Yin Wood is present in the Hour Stem. In 1988 (Yang Earth Dragon year), she was inducted into the Rock and Roll Hall of Fame. In 2016 (Yang Fire Monkey year), Ross received the Presidential Medal of Freedom.

Example 3.50

David Gilmour, English Musician *Pink Floyd*,
March 6, 1946, 23:00 hours

Hour	Day	Month	Year
丙	庚	辛	丙
Yang Fire	**Yang Metal**	Yin Metal	Yang Fire
子	辰	卯	戌
Rat	Dragon	Rabbit	Dog

Gilmour is a Yang Metal Day Stem. The Seven Killings Yang Fire is present in the Hour Stem. He is the guitarist and co-lead vocalist of the band *Pink Floyd*, which has sold more than 250 million records worldwide.

Example 3.51

Shaun White, American Snowboarder and Skateboarder,
September 3, 1986, 04:37 hours

Hour	Day	Month	Year
戊	庚	丙	丙
Yang Earth	**Yang Metal**	Yang Fire	Yang Fire
寅	戌	申	寅
Tiger	Dog	Monkey	Tiger
丙 **Yang Fire**			

White is a Yang Metal Day Stem. The Seven Killings Yang Fire is hidden in the Tiger Hour Branch. He is a three-time Olympic gold medalist in half-pipe snowboarding.

Example 3.52

Chrissie Hynde, American Singer-Songwriter and Musician
The Pretenders, September 7, 1951, 10:20 hours

Hour	Day	Month	Year
辛	庚	丁	辛
Yin Metal	**Yang Metal**	Yin Fire	Yin Metal
巳	戌	酉	卯
Snake	Dog	Rooster	Rabbit
丙 **Yang Fire**			

Hynde is a Yang Metal Day Stem. The Seven Killings Yang Fire is hidden in the Snake Hour Branch. She is the lead vocalist and guitarist of *The Pretenders*. In 2005 (Yin Wood Rooster), Hynde was inducted into the Rock and Roll Hall of Fame.

Example 3.53

Jean-Paul Gaultier, French Fashion Designer,
April 24, 1952, 19:00 hours

Hour	Day	Month	Year
丙	庚	乙	壬
Yang Fire	**Yang Metal**	Yin Wood	Yang Water
戌	子	巳	辰
Dog	Rat	Snake	Dragon

Gaultier is a Yang Metal Day Stem. The Seven Killings Yang Fire is present in the Hour Stem. In January 2020 (still Yin Earth Pig year), he retired after a 50 year career. Gaultier is known for his unconventional design of motifs.

Example 3.54

Freddy Heineken, Dutch Businessman,
November 4, 1923, 12:00 hours

Hour	Day	Month	Year
甲	辛	壬	癸
Yang Wood	**Yin Metal**	Yang Water	Yin Water
午	巳	戌	亥
Horse	Snake	Dog	Pig
丁 **Yin Fire**			

Heineken is a Yin Metal Day Stem. The Seven Killings Yin Fire is hidden in the Horse Hour Branch. He was the chairman of the board of directors for the brewing company Heineken International from 1971 (Yin Metal Pig year) until 1989 (Yin Earth Snake year).

Example 3.55

Susan Sarandon, American Actress,
October 4, 1946, 14:25 hours

Hour	Day	Month	Year
乙	辛	戊	丙
Yin Wood	**Yin Metal**	Yang Earth	Yang Fire
未	亥	戌	戌
Sheep	Pig	Dog	Dog
丁 **Yin Fire**			

Sarandon is a Yin Metal Day Stem. The Seven Killings Yin Fire is hidden in the Sheep Hour Branch. She is the recipient of several awards, including an Oscar and a SAG (Screen Actors Guild) Award.

Example 3.56

Clint Eastwood, American Actor and Filmmaker, May 31, 1930, 17:35 hours

Hour	Day	Month	Year
丁	辛	壬	庚
Yin Fire	**Yin Metal**	Yang Water	Yang Metal
酉	巳	午	午
Rooster	Snake	Horse	Horse

Eastwood is a Yin Metal Day Stem. The Seven Killings Yin Fire is present in the Hour Stem. Over his eight-decade career, he has won four Oscars and four Golden Globe Awards.

Example 3.57

Sylvester Stallone, American Actor, July 6, 1946, 19:20 hours

Hour	Day	Month	Year
戊	辛	乙	丙
Yang Earth	**Yin Metal**	Yin Wood	Yang Fire
戌	巳	未	戌
Dog	Snake	Sheep	Dog
丁 Yin Fire			

Stallone is a Yin Metal Day Stem. The Seven Killings Yin Fire is hidden in the Dog Hour Branch. He is the only actor in American cinema to have starred in a Number One box office film over six consecutive decades.

Example 3.58

Chuck Norris, American Actor and Martial Artist,
March 10, 1940, 03:30 hours

Hour	Day	Month	Year
壬	壬	己	庚
Yang Water	**Yang Water**	Yin Earth	Yang Metal
寅	子	卯	寅
Tiger	Rat	Rabbit	Tiger
戊 **Yang Earth**			

Norris is a Yang Water Day Stem. The Seven Killings Yang Earth is hidden in the Tiger Hour Branch. He won many martial arts championships before embarking on an acting career.

Example 3.59

Don Henley, American Singer and Musician *Eagles*,
July 22, 1947, 08:30 hours

Hour	Day	Month	Year
甲	壬	丁	丁
Yang Wood	**Yang Water**	Yin Fire	Yin Fire
辰	寅	未	亥
Dragon	Tiger	Sheep	Pig
戊 **Yang Earth**			

Henley is a Yang Water Day Stem. The Seven Killings Yang Earth is hidden in the Dragon Hour Branch. He is a founding member of the *Eagles* and was inducted into the Rock and Roll Hall of Fame in 1998 (Yang Earth Tiger year).

Example 3.60

Sir Anthony Hopkins, Welsh Actor, December 31, 1937, 09:15 hours

Hour	Day	Month	Year
乙	壬	壬	丁
Yin Wood	**Yang Water**	Yang Water	Yin Fire
巳	辰	子	丑
Snake	Dragon	Rat	Ox
戊 **Yang Earth**			

Hopkins is a Yang Water Day Stem. The Seven Killings Yang Earth is hidden in the Snake Hour Branch. In 2020 (Yang Metal Rat year), he became the oldest Best Actor Oscar winner for *The Father*.

Example 3.61

Jane Birkin, English-French Actress and Singer, December 14, 1946, 15:00 hours

Hour	Day	Month	Year
戊	壬	庚	丙
Yang Earth	**Yang Water**	Yang Metal	Yang Fire
申	戌	子	戌
Monkey	Dog	Rat	Dog
戊 **Yang Earth**			

Birkin is a Yang Water Day Stem. The Seven Killings Yang Earth is present in the Hour Stem and also hidden in the Monkey Hour Branch. In addition to her music and film career, Birkin has also lent her name to the Hermes Birkin handbag.

Example 3.62

Robert Redford, American Actor and Director, August 18, 1936, 20:02 hours

Hour	Day	Month	Year
庚	壬	丙	丙
Yang Metal	**Yang Water**	Yang Fire	Yang Fire
戌	申	申	子
Dog	Monkey	Monkey	Rat
戊 **Yang Earth**			

Redford is a Yang Water Day Stem. The Seven Killings Yang Metal is hidden in the Dog Hour Branch. He has received numerous awards, including an Oscar and the Presidential Medal of Freedom.

Example 3.63

Sir Elton John, English Singer-Songwriter and Pianist, March 25, 1947, 02:00 hours

Hour	Day	Month	Year
癸	癸	癸	丁
Yin Water	**Yin Water**	Yin Water	Yin Fire
丑	卯	卯	亥
Ox	Rabbit	Rabbit	Pig
己 **Yin Earth**			

John is a Yin Water Day Stem. The Seven Killings Yin Earth is hidden in the Ox Hour Branch. In a six-decade career in music, John has sold more than 300 million records worldwide.

Example 3.64

Niki Lauda, Austrian Racing Car Driver,
February 22, 1949, 11:02 hours

Hour	Day	Month	Year
戊	癸	丙	己
Yang Earth	**Yin Water**	Yang Fire	Yin Earth
午	未	寅	丑
Horse	Sheep	Tiger	Ox
己 **Yin Earth**			

Lauda is a Yin Water Day Stem. The Seven Killings Yin Earth is hidden in the Horse Hour Branch. He won the Formula One World Drivers Championship three times and the only one to have won for Ferrari and McLaren.

Example 3.65

Catherine Deneuve, French Actress,
October 22, 1943, 13:35 hours

Hour	Day	Month	Year
己	癸	壬	癸
Yin Earth	**Yin Water**	Yang Water	Yin Water
未	丑	戌	未
Sheep	Ox	Dog	Sheep
己 **Yin Earth**			

Deneuve is a Yin Water Day Stem. The Seven Killings Yin Earth is present in the Hour Stem and also hidden in the Sheep Hour Branch. She has won two Cesar Awards and is considered one of the greatest European actresses.

Summary

In summary, what to look for in a chart with regard to the Seven Killings:

1. Seven Killings Sitting on an Earth Branch in the Year Pillar indicates a person born into modest circumstances who was able to improve their social and economic status.
2. Seven Killings Sitting on an Earth Branch in the Hour Pillar indicates good fortune.
3. Seven Killings present in the Hour Pillar indicates a good reputation.

肆

Chapter Four

Chapter Four Eating God

The Eating God is the Output that is of the same polarity as the Day Stem. It brings fame, good reputation, health and children (for women). Table 4.1 indicates the Day Stem with the Eating God.

Table 4.1 Day Stem and Eating God

Day Stem	Eating God
甲 Yang Wood	丙 Yang Fire
乙 Yin Wood	丁 Yin Fire
丙 Yang Fire	戊 Yang Earth
丁 Yin Fire	己 Yin Earth
戊 Yang Earth	庚 Yang Metal
己 Yin Earth	辛 Yin Metal
庚 Yang Metal	壬 Yang Water
辛 Yin Metal	癸 Yin Water
壬 Yang Water	甲 Yang Wood
癸 Yin Water	乙 Yin Wood

Eating God Sitting on the Earth Branch

When the Eating God sits on the Earth Branch within the chart, there is good fortune. It can be located in the Hour, Month or Year Pillar. Table 4.2 lists the Day Stem and the Eating God Sitting on an Earth Branch Pillars.

Table 4.2 Day Stem and Eating God Sitting on the Earth Branch

Day Stem	Eating God on the Earth Branch	Eating God on the Earth Branch
甲 Yang Wood	丙 Yang Fire 辰 Dragon	丙 Yang Fire 戌 Dog
乙 Yin Wood	**丁 Yin Fire** **丑 Ox**	丁 Yin Fire 未 Sheep
丙 Yang Fire	戊 Yang Earth 辰 Dragon	**戊 Yang Earth** **戌 Dog**
丁 Yin Fire	己 Yin Earth 丑 Ox	己 Yin Earth 未 Sheep
戊 Yang Earth	庚 Yang Metal 辰 Dragon	庚 Yang Metal 戌 Dog
己 Yin Earth	辛 Yin Metal 丑 Ox	**辛 Yin Metal** **未 Sheep**
庚 Yang Metal	壬 Yang Water 辰 Dragon	壬 Yang Water 戌 Dog
辛 Yin Metal	癸 Yin Water 丑 Ox	癸 Yin Water 未 Sheep
壬 Yang Water	**甲 Yang Wood** **辰 Dragon**	甲 Yang Wood 戌 Dog
癸 Yin Water	乙 Yin Wood 丑 Ox	乙 Yin Wood 未 Sheep

The Pillars in bold can be present in the Hour Pillar.

The following examples illustrate all the Eating God Sitting on the Earth Branch Pillars.

Example 4.1

John Cameron Mitchell, American Actor and Playwright, April 21, 1963, 03:00 hours DST

Hour	Day	Month	Year
乙	甲	丙	癸
Yin Wood	**Yang Wood**	**Yang Fire**	Yin Water
丑	午	辰	卯
Ox	Horse	**Dragon**	Rabbit

Mitchell is a Yang Wood Day Stem. The Eating God Sitting on the Earth Branch Pillar Yang Fire Dragon is present in the Month. He wrote, directed and starred in *Hedwig and the Angry Inch* in 2001 (Yin Metal Snake year).

Example 4.2

Ilie Nastase, Romanian Tennis Player, July 19, 1946, 07:00 hours

Hour	Day	Month	Year
戊	甲	乙	丙
Yang Earth	**Yang Wood**	Yin Wood	**Yang Fire**
辰	午	未	戌
Dragon	Horse	Sheep	**Dog**

Nastase is a Yang Wood Day Stem. The Eating God Sitting on the Earth Branch Yang Fire Dog is present in the Year. Nastase was the first man to be ranked Number One on the Association of Tennis Professionals (ATP) rankings in 1973 (Yin Water Ox year).

Example 4.3

Nicki Minaj, Trinidadian-American Rapper and Singer, December 8, 1982, 09:25 hours

Hour	Day	Month	Year
丁	乙	辛	壬
Yin Fire	**Yin Wood**	Yin Metal	Yang Water
丑	丑	亥	戌
Ox	Ox	Pig	Dog

Minaj is a Yin Wood Day Stem. The Eating God Sitting on the Earth Branch Yin Fire Ox is present in the Hour. Minaj is cited as the "Queen of Rap" and has sold more than 100 million records worldwide.

Example 4.4

John Wayne, American Actor, May 26, 1907, 09:56 hours

Hour	Day	Month	Year
辛	乙	乙	丁
Yin Metal	**Yin Wood**	Yin Wood	**Yin Fire**
巳	亥	巳	未
Snake	Pig	Snake	**Sheep**

Wayne is a Yin Wood Day Stem. The Eating God Sitting on the Earth Branch Pillar Yin Fire Sheep is present in the Year Pillar. Wayne starred in 142 movies over a six-decade career.

Example 4.5

Keshia Knight Pulliam, American Actress, April 9, 1979, 19:32 hours

Hour	Day	Month	Year
戊	丙	戊	己
Yang Earth	**Yang Fire**	**Yang Earth**	Yin Earth
戌	午	辰	未
Dog	Horse	**Dragon**	Sheep

Knight Pulliam is a Yang Fire Day Stem. Two different Eating God Sitting on the Earth Branch Pillars are present in her chart: Yang Earth Dragon in the Month and Yang Earth Dog in the Hour. Knight Pulliam became a child star on *The Cosby Show* from 1984 (Yang Wood Rat year) to 1992 (Yang Water Monkey year).

Example 4.6

Thaksin Shinawatra, Thai Prime Minister 2001 to 2006, July 26, 1949, 12:20 hours

Hour	Day	Month	Year
丙	丁	壬	己
Yang Fire	**Yin Fire**	Yang Water	**Yin Earth**
午	巳	申	丑
Horse	Snake	Monkey	**Ox**

Shinawatra is a Yin Fire Day Stem. The Eating God Sitting on the Earth Branch Yin Earth Ox is present in the Year. Shinawatra was the Prime Minister of Thailand from 2001 (Yin Metal Snake year) to 2006 (Yang Fire Dog year).

Example 4.7

Cat Stevens, British Singer-Songwriter and Musician,
July 21, 1948, 12:01 hours

Hour	Day	Month	Year
丙	丁	己	戊
Yang Fire	**Yin Fire**	**Yin Earth**	Yang Earth
午	未	未	子
Horse	Sheep	**Sheep**	Rat

Stevens is a Yin Fire Day Stem. The Eating God Sitting on the Earth Branch Yin Earth Sheep is present in the Month. Stevens is an accomplished songwriter, known for his classic hits such as *The First Cut is the Deepest, Father and Son* and *Morning has Broken*.

Example 4.8

Al Pacino, American Actor and Filmmaker,
April 25, 1940, 11:02 hours

Hour	Day	Month	Year
戊	戊	庚	庚
Yang Earth	**Yang Earth**	**Yang Metal**	**Yang Metal**
午	戌	辰	辰
Horse	Dog	**Dragon**	**Dragon**

Pacino is a Yang Earth Day Stem. The Eating God Sitting on the Earth Branch Pillar Yang Metal Dragon is present in the Month and Year. Pacino is considered one of the most influential actors of the 20th century, having won an Oscar, two Tony Awards and two Emmy Awards.

Example 4.9

Saif Ali Khan, Indian Actor, August 16, 1970, 04:02 hours

Hour	Day	Month	Year
甲	戊	甲	庚
Yang Wood	**Yang Earth**	Yang Wood	**Yang Metal**
寅	辰	申	戌
Tiger	Dragon	Monkey	**Dog**

Khan is a Yang Earth Day Stem. The Eating God Sitting on the Earth Branch Pillar Yang Metal Dog is present in the Year. A prominent actor in Bollywood Films, Khan has won a National Film Award and seven Fanfare Awards.

Example 4.10

Marlene Dietrich, German-American Actress and Singer, December 27, 1901, 21:15 hours

Hour	Day	Month	Year
乙	己	庚	辛
Yin Wood	**Yin Earth**	Yang Metal	**Yin Metal**
亥	卯	子	丑
Pig	Rabbit	Rat	**Ox**

Dietrich is a Yin Earth Day Stem. The Eating God Sitting on the Earth Branch Pillar Yin Metal Ox is present in the Year. Dietrich had a seven-decade career and was one of the highest paid actresses of the 1930s.

Example 4.11

Ryan Gosling, Canadian Actor,
November 12, 1980, 14:34 hours

Hour	Day	Month	Year
辛	己	丁	庚
Yin Metal	**Yin Earth**	Yin Fire	Yang Metal
未	丑	亥	申
Sheep	Ox	Pig	Monkey

Gosling is a Yin Earth Day Stem. The Eating God Sitting on the Earth Branch Pillar Yin Metal Sheep is present in the Hour. Gosling has received a Golden Globe Award and his movies have grossed 1.9 billion USD.

Example 4.12

Queen Elizabeth 2, British Royalty,
April 21, 1926, 02:40 hours

Hour	Day	Month	Year
丁	庚	壬	丙
Yin Fire	**Yang Metal**	**Yang Water**	Yang Fire
丑	辰	辰	寅
Ox	Dragon	**Dragon**	Tiger

Elizabeth is a Yang Metal Day Stem. The Eating God Sitting on the Earth Branch Pillar Yang Water Dragon is present in the Month. Elizabeth is the longest reigning British monarch, celebrating 70 years on the throne in 2022 (Yang Water Tiger year).

Example 4.13

Li Na, Chinese Tennis Player,
February 26, 1982, 14:30 hours

Hour	Day	Month	Year
癸	庚	癸	壬
Yin Water	**Yang Metal**	Yin Water	**Yang Water**
未	辰	卯	戌
Sheep	Dragon	Rabbit	**Dog**

Li is a Yang Metal Day Stem. The Eating God Sitting on the Earth Branch Yang Water Dog is present in the Year. Li became the first player from Asia to win a Grand Slam, the French Open, in 2011 (Yin Metal Rabbit year).

Example 4.14

Carles Puigdemont, Spanish Politician and Journalist,
December 29, 1962, 22:30 hours

Hour	Day	Month	Year
己	辛	癸	壬
Yin Earth	**Yin Metal**	**Yin Water**	Yang Water
亥	丑	丑	寅
Pig	Ox	**Ox**	Tiger

Puigdemont is a Yin Metal Day Stem. The Eating God Sitting on the Earth Branch Yin Water Ox is present in the Month. Puigdemont was the 130th President of Catalonia from 2016 (Yang Fire Monkey year) to 2017 (Yin Fire Rooster year).

Example 4.15

Sir Ringo Starr, English Singer-Songwriter and Musician *Beatles*, July 7, 1940, 00:05 hours

Hour	Day	Month	Year
戊	辛	癸	庚
Yang Earth	**Yin Metal**	**Yin Water**	Yang Metal
子	亥	未	辰
Rat	Pig	**Sheep**	Dragon

Starr is a Yin Metal Day Stem. The Eating God Sitting on the Earth Branch Pillar Yin Water Sheep is in the Month. Starr was the drummer for *The Beatles* and in 2020 (Yang Metal Rat year), was cited as the wealthiest drummer in the world.

Example 4.16

Oliver Stone, American Film Director, September 15, 1946, 09:58 hours DST

Hour	Day	Month	Year
甲	壬	丁	丙
Yang Wood	**Yang Water**	Yin Fire	Yang Fire
辰	辰	酉	戌
Dragon	Dragon	Rooster	Dog

Stone is a Yang Water Day Stem. The Eating God Sitting on the Earth Branch Pillar Yang Wood Dragon is present in the Hour. Stone has won four Oscars, including two for directing *Platoon* and *Born on the 4th of July*.

Example 4.17

Chico Bouchiki, French Musician *Gipsy Kings*,
October 13, 1954, 04:00 hours

Hour	Day	Month	Year
壬	壬	甲	甲
Yang Water	**Yang Water**	**Yang Wood**	Yang Wood
寅	寅	戌	午
Tiger	Tiger	**Dog**	Horse

Bouchiki is a Yang Water Day Stem. The Eating God Sitting on the Earth Branch Pillar Yang Wood Dog is present in the Month. Bouchiki was a member of *The Gipsy Kings* from 1982 (Yang Water Dog year) to 1992 (Yang Water Rat year).

Example 4.18

Melanie Chisholm, English Singer-Songwriter *Spice Girls*,
January 12, 1974, 21:32 hours

Hour	Day	Month	Year
癸	癸	乙	甲
Yin Water	**Yin Water**	**Yin Wood**	Yang Wood
亥	丑	丑	寅
Pig	Ox	**Ox**	Tiger

Chisholm is a Yin Water Day Stem. The Eating God Sitting on the Earth Branch Pillar Yin Wood Ox is in the Month. Chisholm is a member of the *Spice Girls* and has scored 12 UK Number One Singles solo or as part of a group.

Example 4.19

Donatella Versace, Italian Fashion Designer and Businesswoman, May 2, 1955, 05:00 hours

Hour	Day	Month	Year
乙	癸	庚	乙
Yin Wood	**Yin Water**	Yang Metal	**Yin Wood**
卯	亥	辰	未
Rabbit	Pig	Dragon	**Sheep**

Versace is a Yin Water Day Stem. The Eating God Sitting on the Earth Branch Pillar Yin Wood Sheep is in the Year. Versace became the creative director of fashion company *Versace* following the death of her brother Gianni in 1997 (Yin Fire Ox year).

Eating God Combination Pillar

The Eating God Combination Pillar is present when the Eating God of the Day Stem sits on a Branch that has a Hidden Stem that combines with the Eating God. The Eating God Combination Pillar indicates success.

For a Yin Fire Day Stem, the Eating God is Yin Earth. When the Yin Earth sits on a Pig, the Yang Wood Stem hidden within the Pig combines with Yin Earth. For a Yin Fire Day Stem, Yin Earth Pig is the Eating God Combination Pillar.

For a Yang Metal Day Stem, the Eating God is Yang Water. When the Yang Water sits on a Horse, the Yin Fire Stem hidden within the Horse combines with the Yang Water. When the Yang Water sits on a Dog, the Yin Fire Stem hidden within the Dog also combines with the Yang Water. For a Yang Metal Day Stem, there are two Eating God Combination Pillars, Yang Water Horse and Yang Water Dog.

Table 4.3 indicates the Day Stem, Eating God, Combination Branch and the Hidden Stem within the Branch.

Table 4.3 Day Stem, Eating God, Combination Branch and the Hidden Stem within the Branch

Day Stem	Eating God	Combination Branch	Hidden Stem within Branch
甲 Yang Wood	丙 Yang Fire	戌 Dog	辛 Yin Metal
乙 Yin Wood	丁 Yin Fire	亥 Pig	壬 Yang Water
丙 Yang Fire	戊 Yang Earth	子 Rat	癸 Yin Water
丙 Yang Fire	戊 Yang Earth	辰 Dragon	癸 Yin Water
丁 Yin Fire	己 Yin Earth	亥 Pig	甲 Yang Wood
戊 Yang Earth	庚 Yang Metal	辰 Dragon	乙 Yin Wood
己 Yin Earth	辛 Yin Metal	巳 Snake	丙 Yang Fire
庚 Yang Metal	壬 Yang Water	午 Horse	丁 Yin Fire
庚 Yang Metal	壬 Yang Water	戌 Dog	丁 Yin Fire
辛 Yin Metal	癸 Yin Water	巳 Snake	戊 Yang Earth
壬 Yang Water	甲 Yang Wood	午 Horse	己 Yin Earth
癸 Yin Water	乙 Yin Wood	巳 Snake	庚 Yang Metal

Table 4.4 lists the Day Stem with the corresponding Eating God Combination Pillar.

Table 4.4 Day Stem and Eating God Combination Pillar

Day Stem	Eating God Combination Pillar
甲 Yang Wood	丙 Yang Fire 戌 Dog
乙 Yin Wood	**丁 Yin Fire** **亥 Pig**
丙 Yang Fire	戊 **Yang Earth** 戊 Yang Earth 子 **Rat** 辰 Dragon

丁 Yin Fire	己 Yin Earth 亥 Pig
戊 Yang Earth	庚 Yang Metal 辰 Dragon
己 Yin Earth	辛 Yin Metal 巳 Snake
庚 Yang Metal	**壬 Yang Water** 壬 Yang Water **午 Horse** 戌 Dog
辛 Yin Metal	**癸 Yin Water** **巳 Snake**
壬 Yang Water	甲 Yang Wood 午 Horse
癸 Yin Water	乙 Yin Wood 巳 Snake

The Pillars that are in bold can occur in the Hour Pillar.

The following examples illustrate all the Eating God Combination Pillars.

Example 4.20

Sally Field, American Actress,
November 6, 1946, 04:23 hours

Hour	Day	Month	Year
丙	甲	己	丙
Yang Fire	**Yang Wood**	Yin Earth	**Yang Fire**
寅	子	亥	戌
Tiger	Rat	Pig	**Dog**

Field is a Yang Wood Day Stem. The Eating God Combination Pillar Yang Fire Dog is present in the Year. Field has won two Oscars for Best Actress, for *Norma Rae* and *Places in the Heart*.

Example 4.21

Lenny Kravitz, American Singer and Actor, May 26, 1964, 22:11 hours

Hour	Day	Month	Year
丁	乙	己	甲
Yin Fire	**Yin Wood**	Yin Earth	Yang Wood
亥	亥	巳	辰
Pig	Pig	Snake	Dragon

Kravitz is a Yin Wood Day Stem. The Eating God Combination Pillar Yin Fire Pig is present in the Hour. Kravitz won the Grammy for Best Male Rock Vocal for four consecutive years from 1999 (Yin Earth Rabbit year) to 2002 (Yang Water Horse year).

Example 4.22

Marti Pellow, Scottish Singer *Wet Wet Wet*, March 23, 1965, 00:15 hours

Hour	Day	Month	Year
戊	丙	己	乙
Yang Earth	**Yang Fire**	Yin Earth	Yin Wood
子	子	卯	巳
Rat	Rat	Rabbit	Snake

Pellow is a Yang Fire Day Stem. The Eating God Combination Pillar Yang Earth Rat is present in the Hour. He was the lead singer of *Wet Wet Wet*, which topped the UK Singles Chart for 15 weeks with *Love is All Around*.

Example 4.23

Jake Gyllenhaal, American Actor,
December 19, 1980, 20:08 hours

Hour	Day	Month	Year
戊	丙	戊	庚
Yang Earth	**Yang Fire**	**Yang Earth**	Yang Metal
戌	寅	子	申
Dog	Tiger	**Rat**	Monkey

Gyllenhaal is a Yang Fire Day Stem. The Eating God Combination Pillar Yang Earth Rat is present in the Month. Gyllenhaal has been a leading actor in Hollywood since his breakthrough role in *Donnie Darko* in 2001 (Yin Metal Snake year).

Example 4.24

Val Kilmer, American Actor,
December 31, 1959, 07:58 hours

Hour	Day	Month	Year
甲	丁	丁	己
Yang Wood	**Yin Fire**	Yin Fire	**Yin Earth**
辰	亥	丑	亥
Dragon	Pig	Ox	**Pig**

Kilmer is a Yin Fire Day Stem. The Eating God Combination Pillar Yin Earth Pig is present in the Year. Kilmer found fame with his performance in *Top Gun* in 1986 (Yang Fire Tiger year).

Example 4.25

Stevie Wonder, American Singer and Musician, May 13, 1950, 16:15 hours

Hour	Day	Month	Year
庚	戊	庚	庚
Yang Metal	**Yang Earth**	**Yang Metal**	Yang Metal
申	申	辰	寅
Monkey	Monkey	**Dragon**	Tiger

Wonder is a Yang Earth Day Stem. The Eating God Combination Pillar Yang Metal Dragon is present in the Month. Wonder has won 25 Grammys, the most by a solo artist.

Example 4.26

Ronald Isley, American Singer-Songwriter, May 21, 1941, 07:25 hours

Hour	Day	Month	Year
戊	己	癸	辛
Yang Earth	**Yin Earth**	Yin Water	**Yin Metal**
辰	巳	巳	巳
Dragon	Snake	Snake	**Snake**

Isley is a Yin Earth Day Stem. The Eating God Combination Pillar Yin Metal Snake is present in the Year. Isley is the lead singer and founding member of the family group *The Isley Brothers*.

Example 4.27

Agnetha Faltskog, Swedish Singer and Actress *ABBA*,
April 5, 1950, 12:35 hours

Hour	Day	Month	Year
壬	庚	己	庚
Yang Water	**Yang Metal**	Yin Earth	Yang Metal
午	午	卯	寅
Horse	Horse	Rabbit	Tiger

Faltskog is a Yang Metal Day Stem. The Eating God Combination Pillar Yang Water Horse is present in the Hour. Faltskog is a member of *ABBA*, which has sold more than 380 million records worldwide.

Example 4.28

Tony Parker, French-American Basketball Player,
May 17, 1982, 16:40 hours

Hour	Day	Month	Year
甲	庚	乙	壬
Yang Wood	**Yang Metal**	Yin Wood	**Yang Water**
申	子	巳	戌
Monkey	Rat	Snake	**Dog**

Parker is a Yang Metal Day Stem. The Eating God Combination Pillar Yang Water Dog is present in the Year. Parker has won four National Basketball Association NBA Championships with his team the *San Antonio Spurs*.

Example 4.29

Eminem, American Rapper,
October 17, 1972, 11:04 hours DST

Hour	Day	Month	Year
癸	辛	庚	壬
Yin Water	**Yin Metal**	Yang Metal	Yang Water
巳	巳	戌	子
Snake	Snake	Dog	Rat

Eminem is a Yin Metal Day Stem. The Eating God Combination Pillar Yin Water Snake is present in the Hour. Eminem has sold more than 220 million records and was inducted into the Rock and Roll Hall of Fame in 2022 (Yang Water Tiger year).

Example 4.30

Chris Evans, American Actor, June 13, 1981, 18:16 hours

Hour	Day	Month	Year
己	壬	甲	辛
Yin Earth	**Yang Water**	**Yang Wood**	Yin Metal
酉	戌	午	酉
Rooster	Dog	**Horse**	Rooster

Evans is a Yang Water Day Stem. The Eating God Combination Pillar Yang Wood Horse is present in the Month. Evans is known for portraying Captain America in the Marvel films.

Example 4.31

Kirsten Dunst, American Actress,
April 30, 1982, 13:00 hours DST

Hour	Day	Month	Year
戊	癸	乙	壬
Yang Earth	**Yin Water**	**Yin Wood**	Yang Water
午	未	巳	戌
Horse	Sheep	**Snake**	Dog

Dunst is a Yin Water Day Stem. The Eating God Combination Pillar Yin Wood Snake is present in the Month. She won a Cannes Film Festival Award for Best Actress for *Melancholia* in 2011 (Yin Metal Rabbit year).

Eating God Sitting on the Birth Branch

When the Eating God is Sitting on its Birth Branch (as determined by the Three Harmony Life Stages), then there is the potential for fame and success. There are five Yang Eating God Stems and five Yin Eating God Stems to consider.

The Eating God is the same polarity as the Day Stem. For Yang Day Stems, consider Table 4.5 and for Yin Day Stems, look up Table 4.6.

Table 4.5 Lists the 12 Life Stages for the Eating God Yang Stems. The Life Stage to take into account is the Birth, which has been highlighted. Note that Yang Wood and Yang Metal Eating God Stems cannot sit on the Birth Branch as they are of the opposite polarity.

Table 4.5 12 Life Stages for the Eating God Yang Stems

Stem Life Stage	甲 Yang Wood	丙 Yang Fire	戊 Yang Earth	庚 Yang Metal	壬 Yang Water
Birth	亥 Pig	寅 Tiger	寅 Tiger	巳 Snake	申 Monkey
Bath	子 Rat	卯 Rabbit	卯 Rabbit	午 Horse	酉 Rooster
Attire	丑 Ox	辰 Dragon	辰 Dragon	未 Sheep	戌 Dog
Arrival	寅 Tiger	巳 Snake	巳 Snake	申 Monkey	亥 Pig
Peak	卯 Rabbit	午 Horse	午 Horse	酉 Rooster	子 Rat
Ageing	辰 Dragon	未 Sheep	未 Sheep	戌 Dog	丑 Ox
Sickness	巳 Snake	申 Monkey	申 Monkey	亥 Pig	寅 Tiger
Death	午 Horse	酉 Rooster	酉 Rooster	子 Rat	卯 Rabbit
Tomb	未 Sheep	戌 Dog	戌 Dog	丑 Ox	辰 Dragon
End	申 Monkey	亥 Pig	亥 Pig	寅 Tiger	巳 Snake
Conception	酉 Rooster	子 Rat	子 Rat	卯 Rabbit	午 Horse
Nurture	戌 Dog	丑 Ox	丑 Ox	辰 Dragon	未 Sheep

Table 4.6 lists the 12 Life Stages for Eating God Yin Stems. The Life Stage to take into account is the Birth, which has been highlighted. Note that the Yin Wood and Yin Metal Eating God Stems do not sit on the Birth Branch as they are of the opposite polarity.

Table 4.6 12 Life Stages for the Eating God Yin Stems

Stem Life Stage	乙 Yin Wood	丁 Yin Fire	己 Yin Earth	辛 Yin Metal	癸 Yin Water
Birth	午 Horse	酉 Rooster	酉 Rooster	子 Rat	卯 Rabbit
Bath	巳 Snake	申 Monkey	申 Monkey	亥 Pig	寅 Tiger
Attire	辰 Dragon	未 Sheep	未 Sheep	戌 Dog	丑 Ox
Arrival	卯 Rabbit	午 Horse	午 Horse	酉 Rooster	子 Rat
Peak	寅 Tiger	巳 Snake	巳 Snake	申 Monkey	亥 Pig
Ageing	丑 Ox	辰 Dragon	辰 Dragon	未 Sheep	戌 Dog
Sickness	子 Rat	卯 Rabbit	卯 Rabbit	午 Horse	酉 Rooster
Death	亥 Pig	寅 Tiger	寅 Tiger	巳 Snake	申 Monkey
Tomb	戌 Dog	丑 Ox	丑 Ox	辰 Dragon	未 Sheep
End	酉 Rooster	子 Rat	子 Rat	卯 Rabbit	午 Horse
Conception	申 Monkey	亥 Pig	亥 Pig	寅 Tiger	巳 Snake
Nurture	未 Sheep	戌 Dog	戌 Dog	丑 Ox	辰 Dragon

Table 4.7 lists the Day Stem and Eating God Sitting on Birth Branch Pillar

Table 4.7 Day Stem and Eating God Sitting on the Birth Branch Pillar

Day Stem	Eating God Sitting on the Birth Branch
甲 Yang Wood	**丙 Yang Fire** **寅 Tiger**
乙 Yin Wood	丁 Yin Fire 酉 Rooster
丙 Yang Fire	戊 Yang Earth 寅 Tiger
丁 Yin Fire	**己 Yin Earth** **酉 Rooster**
戊 Yang Earth	
己 Yin Earth	
庚 Yang Metal	壬 Yang Water 申 Monkey
辛 Yin Metal	癸 Yin Water 卯 Rabbit
壬 Yang Water	
癸 Yin Water	

The Pillars that have been highlighted can also occur in the Hour Pillar.

Example 4.32

Sir Cameron Mackintosh, British Theatrical Producer, October 17, 1946, 04:30 hours

Hour	Day	Month	Year
丙	甲	戊	丙
Yang Fire	**Yang Wood**	Yang Earth	Yang Fire
寅	子	戌	戌
Tiger	Rat	Dog	Dog

Mackintosh is a Yang Wood Day Stem. The Eating God Sitting on the Birth Branch Pillar Yang Fire Tiger is present in the Hour. Two of Mackintosh's musical productions, *Les Miserables* and *The Phantom of the Opera* are two of the longest running musicals in London's West End.

Example 4.33

Gustavo Kuerten, Brazilian Tennis Player, September 10, 1976, 03:30 hours

Hour	Day	Month	Year
戊	乙	丁	丙
Yang Earth	**Yin Wood**	**Yin Fire**	Yang Fire
寅	丑	酉	辰
Tiger	Ox	**Rooster**	Dragon

Kuerten is a Yin Wood Day Stem. The Eating God Sitting on the Birth Branch Pillar Yin Fire Rooster is present in the Month. Kuerten was ranked Number One on the Men's Tennis Rankings in 2000 (Yang Metal Dragon year).

Example 4.34

Karen Carpenter, American Singer and Drummer, March 2, 1950, 11:45 hours

Hour	Day	Month	Year
甲	丙	戊	庚
Yang Wood	**Yang Fire**	**Yang Earth**	Yang Metal
午	申	寅	寅
Horse	Monkey	**Tiger**	Tiger

Carpenter is a Yang Fire Day Stem. The Eating God Sitting on the Birth Branch Pillar Yang Earth Tiger is present in the Month. As part of *The Carpenters*, she scored three US Number One Singles and sold more than 90 million records.

Example 4.35

Sir Sean Connery, Scottish Actor, August 25, 1930, 18:05 hours

Hour	Day	Month	Year
己	丁	甲	庚
Yin Earth	**Yin Fire**	Yang Wood	Yang Metal
酉	未	申	午
Rooster	Sheep	Monkey	Horse

Connery is a Yin Fire Day Stem. The Eating God Sitting on the Birth Branch Pillar Yin Earth Rooster is present in the Hour. Connery was the first actor to portray fictional British secret agent James Bond in 1962 (Yang Water Tiger year).

Example 4.36

Keith Carradine, American Actor and Singer, August 8, 1949, 00:47 hours

Hour	Day	Month	Year
丙	庚	壬	己
Yang Fire	**Yang Metal**	**Yang Water**	Yin Earth
子	午	申	丑
Rat	Horse	**Monkey**	Ox

Carradine is a Yang Metal Day Stem. The Eating God Sitting on the Birth Branch Pillar Yang Water Monkey is present in the Month. He has enjoyed a six-decade career on the screen and stage.

Example 4.37

Conan O'Brien, American Television Host and Comedian, April 18, 1963, 13:48 hours

Hour	Day	Month	Year
乙	辛	丙	癸
Yin Wood	**Yin Metal**	Yang Fire	**Yin Water**
未	卯	辰	卯
Sheep	Rabbit	Dragon	**Rabbit**

O'Brien is a Yin Metal Day Stem. The Eating God Sitting on the Birth Branch Pillar Yin Water Rabbit is present in the Year. O'Brien is noted for hosting late-night talk shows for almost three decades, having started in 1993 (Yin Water Rooster year).

Eating God in Stem Combination

When the Eating God is involved in a Stem Combination within the chart, there is success. The following examples illustrate the Eating God in a Stem Combination for all Day Stems.

Example 4.38

Jerry Lewis, American Actor and Comedian, March 16, 1926, 12:15 hours

Hour	Day	Month	Year
庚	甲	辛	丙
Yang Metal	**Yang Wood**	**Yin Metal**	**Yang Fire**
午	辰	卯	寅
Horse	Dragon	Rabbit	Tiger

Lewis is a Yang Wood Day Stem. The Eating God Yang Fire is present in the Year Pillar and is involved in a Stem Combination with Yin Metal in the Month. Nicknamed the King of Comedy, Lewis is recognized as one of the most significant cultural figures of the 20th century.

Example 4.39

Laura Dern, American Actress, February 10, 1967, 07:48 hours

Hour	Day	Month	Year
庚	乙	壬	丁
Yang Metal	**Yin Wood**	**Yang Water**	**Yin Fire**
辰	巳	寅	未
Dragon	Snake	Tiger	Sheep

Dern is a Yin Wood Day Stem. The Eating God Yin Fire in the Year is involved in a Stem Combination with Yang Water in the Month. Dern has enjoyed a four-decade career and won an Oscar for Best Supporting Actress for *Marriage Story* in 2020 (Yang Metal Rat year).

Example 4.40

Randy Couture, American Wrestler and Actor, June 22, 1963

Hour	Day	Month	Year
	丙	戊	癸
	Yang Fire	**Yang Earth**	**Yin Water**
	申	午	卯
	Monkey	Horse	Rabbit

Couture is a Yang Fire Day Stem. The Eating God Yang Earth in the Month is involved in a Stem Combination with Yin Water in the Year. Couture has had careers as a US Army Sergeant, mixed martial artist and wrestler before becoming an actor.

Example 4.41

Dakota Johnson, American Actress and Model, October 4, 1989, 14:49 hours

Hour	Day	Month	Year
丁	丁	甲	己
Yin Fire	**Yin Fire**	Yang Wood	Yin Earth
未	酉	戌	巳
Sheep	Rooster	Dog	Snake

Johnson is a Yin Fire Day Stem. The Eating God Yin Earth in the Year is involved in a Stem Combination with Yang Wood in the Month. Johnson had her breakthrough role in *Fifty Shades of Grey* in 2015 (Yin Wood Sheep year).

Example 4.42

Robert Downey Jr., American Actor, April 4, 1965, 13:10 hours

Hour	Day	Month	Year
己	戊	庚	乙
Yin Earth	**Yang Earth**	Yang Metal	Yin Wood
未	子	辰	巳
Sheep	Rat	Dragon	Snake

Downey is a Yang Earth Day Stem. The Eating God Yang Metal in the Month is involved in a Stem Combination with Yin Wood in the Year. Downey has had a four-decade career highlighted by his roles as Iron Man and Sherlock Holmes in the movies.

Example 4.43

Freddie Prinze Jr., American Actor,
March 8, 1976, 19:38 hours

Hour	Day	Month	Year
甲	己	辛	丙
Yang Wood	**Yin Earth**	**Yin Metal**	**Yang Fire**
戌	未	卯	辰
Dog	Sheep	Rabbit	Dragon

Prinze is a Yin Earth Day Stem. The Eating God Yin Metal in the Month is involved in a Stem Combination with Yang Fire in the Year. Prinze had his first major starring role in *I Know What You Did Last Summer* in 1997 (Yin Fire Ox year).

Example 4.44

Loreena McKennit, Canadian Singer and Musician,
February 17, 1957, 19:00 hours

Hour	Day	Month	Year
丙	庚	壬	丁
Yang Fire	**Yang Metal**	**Yang Water**	**Yin Fire**
戌	申	寅	酉
Dog	Monkey	Tiger	Rooster

McKennit is a Yang Metal Day Stem. The Eating God Yang Water in the Month is involved in a Stem Combination with Yin Fire in the Year. McKennit is known for her soprano voice and has sold more than 14 million records worldwide.

Example 4.45

Greg Kinnear, American Actor, June 17, 1963, 15:21 hours

Hour	Day	Month	Year
丙	辛	戊	癸
Yang Fire	**Yin Metal**	**Yang Earth**	**Yin Water**
申	卯	午	卯
Monkey	Rabbit	Horse	Rabbit

Kinnear is a Yin Metal Day Stem. The Eating God Yin Water in the Year is involved in a Stem Combination with Yang Earth in the Month. Kinnear received an Oscar nomination for Best Supporting Actor for *As Good as It Gets* in 1997 (Yin Fire Ox year).

Example 4.46

Bonnie Raitt, American Singer and Guitarist, November 8, 1949, 16:08 hours

Hour	Day	Month	Year
戊	壬	甲	己
Yang Earth	**Yang Water**	**Yang Wood**	**Yin Earth**
申	寅	戌	丑
Monkey	Tiger	Dog	Ox

Raitt is a Yang Water Day Stem. The Eating God Yang Wood in the Month is involved in a Stem Combination with Yin Earth in the Year. Raitt has won ten Grammy Awards and was inducted into the Rock and Roll Hall of Fame in 2000 (Yang Metal Dragon year).

Example 4.47

Ritchie Blackmore, English Singer and Guitarist *Deep Purple*, April 14, 1945, 00:10 hours

Hour	Day	Month	Year
壬	癸	庚	乙
Yang Water	**Yin Water**	**Yang Metal**	**Yin Wood**
子	丑	辰	酉
Rat	Ox	Dragon	Rooster

Blackmore has a Yin Water Day Stem. The Eating God Yin Wood is involved in a Stem Combination with Yang Metal in the Month. Blackmore is the guitarist for *Deep Purple* and was inducted into the Rock and Roll Hall of Fame in 2016 (Yang Fire Monkey year) as part of the band.

Summary

In summary, what to look for in a chart with regard to the Eating God:

1. Eating God Sitting on the Earth Branch.
2. Eating God Combination Pillar.
3. Eating God Sitting on the Birth Branch.
4. Eating God in a Stem Combination.

伍

Chapter Five

Chapter Five Hurting Officer

The Hurting Officer is the Output of the opposite polarity as the Day Stem. While it may be associated with fame, ranking, glamour and talent and is commonly seen in performing artists, it may also create issues. It undermines the function and strength of the Power element.

Table 5.1 indicates the Day Stem and the Hurting Officer.

Table 5.1 Day Stem and Hurting Officer

Day Stem	Hurting Officer
甲 Yang Wood	丁 Yin Fire
乙 Yin Wood	丙 Yang Fire
丙 Yang Fire	己 Yin Earth
丁 Yin Fire	戊 Yang Earth
戊 Yang Earth	辛 Yin Metal
己 Yin Earth	庚 Yang Metal
庚 Yang Metal	癸 Yin Water
辛 Yin Metal	壬 Yang Water
壬 Yang Water	乙 Yin Wood
癸 Yin Water	甲 Yang Wood

Hurting Officer Sitting on the Resource

When the Hurting Officer is Sitting on a Branch where one of the Hidden Stems contains the Resource for the Day Stem, there will be success and achievement.

Table 5.2 lists the Day Stem and the Hurting Office Sitting on the Resource Pillars.

Table 5.2 Day Stem and Hurting Officer Sitting on the Resource Pillars

Day Stem	Hurting Officer Sitting on the Resource Pillars
甲 Yang Wood	丁 Yin Fire　丁 Yin Fire 丑 Ox　　　亥 Pig
乙 Yin Wood	**丙 Yang Fire** 丙 Yang Fire 丙 Yang Fire **子 Rat**　　　辰 Dragon　　申 Monkey
丙 Yang Fire	**己 Yin Earth** 己 Yin Earth 己 Yin Earth **亥 Pig**　　　卯 Rabbit　　未 Sheep
丁 Yin Fire	戊 Yang Earth 戊 Yang Earth 寅 Tiger　　　辰 Dragon
戊 Yang Earth	辛 Yin Metal 辛 Yin Metal 巳 Snake　　未 Sheep
己 Yin Earth	庚 Yang Metal **庚 Yang Metal** 庚 Yang Metal 寅 Tiger　　　**午 Horse**　　戌 Dog
庚 Yang Metal	癸 Yin Water 癸 Yin Water **癸 Yin Water** 丑 Ox　　　巳 Snake　　**未 Sheep**
辛 Yin Metal	壬 Yang Water **壬 Yang Water** 壬 Yang Water 壬 Yang Water 寅 Tiger　　**辰 Dragon**　午 Horse　　申 Monkey 壬 Yang Water 戌 Dog
壬 Yang Water	乙 Yin Wood **乙 Yin Wood** 乙 Yin Wood 丑 Ox　　　**巳 Snake**　　酉 Rooster
癸 Yin Water	甲 Yang Wood 甲 Yang Wood 申 Monkey　戌 Dog

The Pillars in bold can occur in the Hour Pillars.

The following examples illustrate all the Hurting Officer Sitting on the Resource Pillars.

Example 5.1

Dawn Fraser, Australian Swimmer,
September 4, 1937, 06:09 hours

Hour	Day	Month	Year
丁	甲	戊	丁
Yin Fire	**Yang Wood**	Yang Earth	**Yin Fire**
卯	午	申	丑
Rabbit	Horse	Monkey	**Ox**
			癸 **Yin Water**

Fraser is a Yang Wood Day Stem. The Hurting Officer Yin Fire is present in the Year. It sits on an Ox Branch, which contains Yin Water, the Resource for the Yang Wood Day Stem. Fraser is the first of only four swimmers to win individual gold medals for the same event (100 metres freestyle) in three successive Olympics.

Example 5.2

Goldie Hawn, American Actress,
November 21, 1945, 09:20 hours

Hour	Day	Month	Year
己	甲	丁	乙
Yin Earth	**Yang Wood**	**Yin Fire**	Yin Wood
巳	午	亥	酉
Snake	Horse	**Pig**	Rooster
		壬 **Yang Water**	

Hawn is a Yang Wood Day Stem. The Hurting Officer Yin Fire is present in the Month. It sits on a Pig Branch, which contains Yang Water, the Resource for the Yang Wood Day Stem. Hawn has been a star for more than five decades, having won an Oscar for Best Supporting Actress for *Cactus Flower* in 1970 (Yang Metal Dog year).

Example 5.3

Jared Leto, American Actor and Singer, December 26, 1971, 00:00 hours

Hour	Day	Month	Year
丙	乙	庚	辛
Yang Fire	**Yin Wood**	Yang Metal	Yin Metal
子	酉	子	亥
Rat	Rooster	Rat	Pig
癸 **Yin Water**			

Leto is a Yin Wood Day Stem. The Hurting Officer Yang Fire is present in the Hour. It sits on a Rat Branch, which contains Yin Water, the Resource for the Yin Wood Day Stem. Leto won an Oscar for Best Supporting Actor for *The Dallas Buyers Club* in 2014 (Yang Wood Horse year).

Example 5.4

Jean-Paul Belmondo, French Actor, April 9, 1933, 09:00 hours

Hour	Day	Month	Year
辛	乙	丙	癸
Yin Metal	**Yin Wood**	**Yang Fire**	Yin Water
巳	巳	辰	酉
Snake	Snake	**Dragon**	Rooster
		癸 **Yin Water**	

Belmondo is a Yin Wood Day Stem. The Hurting Officer Yang Fire is present in the Month. It sits on a Dragon Branch, which contains Yin Water, the Resource for the Yin Wood Day Stem. Belmondo was a major movie star in France for over 50 years.

Example 5.5

Jimmy Barnes, Australian Singer-Songwriter,
April 28, 1956, 16:30 hours

Hour	Day	Month	Year
甲	乙	壬	丙
Yang Wood	**Yin Wood**	Yang Water	**Yang Fire**
申	丑	辰	申
Monkey	Ox	Dragon	**Monkey**
			壬 **Yang Water**

Barnes is a Yin Wood Day Stem. The Hurting Officer Yang Fire is present in the Year. It sits on a Monkey Branch, which contains Yang Water, the Resource for the Yin Wood Day Stem. Barnes has scored 17 Number One Albums in Australia, the most for an artist in the Australian charts.

Example 5.6

Vincent Cassel, French Actor,
November 23, 1966, 22:30 hours

Hour	Day	Month	Year
己	丙	己	丙
Yin Earth	**Yang Fire**	**Yin Earth**	Yang Fire
亥	戌	亥	午
Pig	Dog	**Pig**	Horse
甲 **Yang Wood**		甲 **Yang Wood**	

Cassel is a Yang Fire Day Stem. The Hurting Officer Yin Earth is present in the Month and Hour. They sit on a Pig Branch each, which contains Yang Wood, the Resource for the Yang Fire Day Stem. Cassel won a Cesar Award for *Mesrine* in 2009 (Yin Earth Ox year).

Example 5.7

Alain Prost, French Racing Driver,
February 24, 1955, 11:45 hours

Hour	Day	Month	Year
甲	丙	己	乙
Yang Wood	**Yang Fire**	**Yin Earth**	Yin Wood
午	辰	卯	未
Horse	Dragon	**Rabbit**	Sheep
		乙 **Yin Wood**	

Prost is a Yang Fire Day Stem. The Hurting Officer Yin Earth is present in the Month. It sits on a Rabbit Branch, which contains Yin Wood, the Resource for the Yang Fire Day Stem. He is a four-time Formula One Drivers' Champion.

Example 5.8

Nelson Mandela, South African President 1994 to 1999,
July 18, 1918, 14:54 hours

Hour	Day	Month	Year
乙	丙	己	戊
Yin Wood	**Yang Fire**	**Yin Earth**	Yang Earth
未	寅	未	午
Sheep	Tiger	**Sheep**	Horse
		乙 **Yin Wood**	

Mandela is a Yang Fire Day Stem. The Hurting Officer Yin Earth is present in the Month. It sits on a Sheep Branch, which contains Yin Wood, the Resource for the Yang Fire Day Stem. Mandela was the first President of South Africa.

Example 5.9

Prince Andrew, Duke of York, British Royalty,
February 19, 1960, 15:30 hours

Hour	Day	Month	Year
戊	丁	戊	庚
Yang Earth	**Yin Fire**	**Yang Earth**	Yang Metal
申	丑	寅	子
Monkey	Ox	**Tiger**	Rat
		甲 **Yang Wood**	

Andrew is a Yin Fire Day Stem. The Hurting Officer Yang Earth is present in the Month. It sits on a Tiger Branch, which contains Yang Wood, the Resource for the Yin Fire Day Stem. Andrew served in the Royal Navy as a helicopter pilot, instructor and as the captain of a warship.

Example 5.10

Robert Stigwood, Australian-British Music Producer and Impresario, April 16, 1934, 03:10 hours

Hour	Day	Month	Year
壬	丁	戊	甲
Yang Water	**Yin Fire**	**Yang Earth**	Yang Wood
寅	巳	辰	戌
Tiger	Snake	**Dragon**	Dog
		乙 **Yin Wood**	

Stigwood is a Yin Fire Day Stem. The Hurting Officer Yang Earth is present in the Month. It sits on a Dragon Branch, which contains Yin Wood, the Resource for the Yin Fire Day Stem. Stigwood produced the hit films *Grease* and *Saturday Night Fever* and managed *The Bee Gees*.

Example 5.11

Tina Fey, American Actress and Comedian,
May 18, 1970, 10:42 hours

Hour	Day	Month	Year
丁	戊	辛	庚
Yin Fire	**Yang Earth**	**Yin Metal**	Yang Metal
巳	戌	巳	戌
Snake	Dog	**Snake**	Dog
		丙 **Yang Fire**	

Fey is a Yang Earth Day Stem. The Hurting Officer Yin Metal is present in the Month. It sits on a Snake Branch, which contains Yang Fire, the Resource for the Yang Earth Day Stem. Fey has won nine Emmys, three Golden Globes, five Screen Actor Guild Awards and seven Writers Guild of America Awards.

Example 5.12

Louis Tomlinson, English Singer *One Direction*,
December 24, 1991, 13:47 hours

Hour	Day	Month	Year
己	戊	庚	辛
Yin Earth	**Yang Earth**	Yang Metal	**Yin Metal**
未	辰	子	未
Sheep	Dragon	Rat	**Sheep**
			丁 **Yin Fire**

Tomlinson is a Yang Earth Day Stem. The Hurting Officer Yin Metal is present in the Year. It sits on a Sheep Branch, which contains Yin Fire, the Resource for the Yang Earth Day Stem. Tomlinson was a member of the boy band *One Direction*, which sold 70 million records.

Example 5.13

Bryce Dallas Howard, American Actress,
March 2, 1981, 07:49 hours

Hour	Day	Month	Year
戊	己	庚	辛
Yang Earth	**Yin Earth**	**Yang Metal**	Yin Metal
辰	卯	寅	酉
Dragon	Rabbit	**Tiger**	Rooster
		丙 **Yang Fire**	

Howard is a Yin Earth Day Stem. The Hurting Officer Yang Metal is present in the Month. It sits on a Tiger Branch, which contains Yang Fire, the Resource for the Yin Earth Day Stem. Howard starred in the *Jurassic World* films.

Example 5.14

Chris Pratt, American Actor, June 21, 1979, 16:31 hours

Hour	Day	Month	Year
壬	己	庚	己
Yang Water	**Yin Earth**	**Yang Metal**	Yin Earth
申	未	午	未
Monkey	Sheep	**Horse**	Sheep
		丁 **Yin Fire**	

Pratt is a Yin Earth Day Stem. The Hurting Officer Yang Metal is present in the Month. It sits on a Horse Branch, which contains Yin Fire, the Resource for the Yin Earth Day Stem. Pratt has starred in *The Guardians of the Galaxy* and *Jurassic World* movies.

Example 5.15

Drew Barrymore, American Actress and Filmmaker,
February 22, 1975, 11:51 hours

Hour	Day	Month	Year
庚	己	戊	乙
Yang Metal	**Yin Earth**	Yang Earth	Yin Wood
午	亥	寅	卯
Horse	Pig	Tiger	Rabbit
丁 **Yin Fire**			

Barrymore is a Yin Earth Day Stem. The Hurting Officer Yang Metal is present in the Hour. It sits on a Horse Branch, which contains Yin Fire, the Resource for the Yin Earth Day Stem. Barrymore achieved fame as a child actress in *E.T. the Extra Terrestrial* in 1982 (Yang Water Dog year).

Example 5.16

Andre Agassi, American Tennis Player,
April 29, 1970, 04:00 hours

Hour	Day	Month	Year
丙	己	庚	庚
Yang Fire	**Yin Earth**	Yang Metal	**Yang Metal**
寅	卯	辰	戌
Tiger	Rabbit	Dragon	**Dog**
			丁 **Yin Fire**

Agassi is a Yin Earth Day Stem. The Hurting Officer Yang Metal is present in the Year. It sits on a Dog Branch, which contains Yin Fire, the Resource for the Yin Earth Day Stem. Agassi is an eight-time tennis major champion and an Olympic gold medalist.

Example 5.17

Vivien Leigh, British Actress,
November 5, 1913, 17:16 hours

Hour	Day	Month	Year
乙	庚	癸	癸
Yin Wood	**Yang Metal**	Yin Water	**Yin Water**
酉	寅	亥	丑
Rooster	Tiger	Pig	**Ox**
			己 **Yin Earth**

Leigh is a Yang Metal Day Stem. The Hurting Officer Yin Water is present in the Year. It sits on an Ox Branch, which contains Yin Earth, the Resource for the Yang Metal Day Stem. Leigh won two Best Actress Oscars, for *Gone with the Wind* and *A Streetcar Named Desire*.

Example 5.18

Megan Fox, American Actress and Model,
May 16, 1986, 00:35 hours

Hour	Day	Month	Year
丙	庚	癸	丙
Yang Fire	**Yang Metal**	**Yin Water**	Yang Fire
子	申	巳	寅
Rat	Monkey	**Snake**	Tiger
		戊 **Yang Earth**	

Fox is a Yang Metal Day Stem. The Hurting Officer Yin Water is present in the Month. It sits on a Snake Branch, which contains Yang Earth, the Resource for the Yang Metal Day Stem. Fox has starred in the *Transformers* and *Teenage Mutant Ninja Turtles* films.

Example 5.19

Renee Zellweger, American Actress, April 25, 1969, 14:41 hours

Hour	Day	Month	Year
癸	庚	戊	己
Yin Water	**Yang Metal**	Yang Earth	Yin Earth
未	午	辰	酉
Sheep	Horse	Dragon	Rooster
己 **Yin Earth**			

Zellweger is a Yang Metal Day Stem. The Hurting Officer Yin Water is present in the Hour. It sits on a Sheep Branch, which contains Yin Earth, the Resource for the Yang Metal Day Stem. Zellweger has won two Oscars, one for Best Supporting Actress for *Cold Mountain* and one for Best Actress for *Judy*.

Example 5.20

Jodie Foster, American Actress and Director, November 19, 1962, 08:14 hours

Hour	Day	Month	Year
壬	辛	辛	壬
Yang Water	**Yin Metal**	Yin Metal	**Yang Water**
辰	酉	亥	寅
Dragon	Rooster	Pig	**Tiger**
戊 **Yang Earth**			戊 **Yang Earth**

Foster is a Yin Metal Day Stem. The Hurting Officer Yang Water is present in the Year and Hour. In the Year, it sits on a Tiger Branch, and in the Hour, it sits on a Dragon Branch, both of which contain Yang Earth, the Resource for the Yin Metal Day Stem. Foster has won two Best Actress Oscars, for *The Accused* and *The Silence of the Lambs*.

Example 5.21

Venus Williams, American Tennis Player, June 17, 1980, 14:12 hours

Hour	Day	Month	Year
乙	辛	壬	庚
Yin Wood	**Yin Metal**	**Yang Water**	Yang Metal
未	酉	午	申
Sheep	Rooster	**Horse**	Monkey
		己 **Yin Earth**	

Williams is a Yin Metal Day Stem. The Hurting Officer Yang Water is present in the Month. It sits on a Horse Branch, which contains Yin Earth, the Resource for the Yin Metal Day Stem. Williams was ranked Number One in both Singles and Doubles in the Women's Tennis rankings and won five Wimbledon singles titles.

Example 5.22

Lily Tomlin, American Actress and Comedian, September 1, 1939, 01:45 hours

Hour	Day	Month	Year
己	辛	壬	己
Yin Earth	**Yin Metal**	**Yang Water**	Yin Earth
丑	丑	申	卯
Ox	Ox	**Monkey**	Rabbit
		戊 **Yang Earth**	

Tomlin is a Yin Metal Day Stem. The Hurting Officer Yang Water is present in the Month. It sits on a Monkey Branch, which contains Yang Earth, the Resource for the Yin Metal Day Stem. Tomlin received the Screen Actors Guild Life Achievement Award in 2017 (Yin Fire Rooster year).

Example 5.23

Doris Day, American Actress and Singer,
April 3, 1922, 16:30 hours

Hour	Day	Month	Year
丙	辛	甲	壬
Yang Fire	**Yin Metal**	Yang Wood	**Yang Water**
申	丑	辰	戌
Monkey	Ox	Dragon	**Dog**
			戊 **Yang Earth**

Day is a Yin Metal Day Stem. The Hurting Officer Yang Water is present in the Year. It sits on a Dog Branch, which contains Yang Earth, the Resource for the Yin Metal Day Stem. Day was one of the biggest film stars from the 1950s to the 1960s.

Example 5.24

Jimmy Page, English Musician and Singer *Led Zeppelin*,
January 9, 1944, 04:00 hours

Hour	Day	Month	Year
壬	壬	乙	癸
Yang Water	**Yang Water**	**Yin Wood**	Yin Water
寅	申	丑	未
Tiger	Monkey	**Ox**	Sheep
		辛 **Yin Metal**	

Page is a Yang Water Day Stem. The Hurting Officer Yin Wood is present in the Month. It sits on an Ox Branch, which contains Yin Metal, the Resource for the Yang Water Day Stem. Page is the guitarist and founding member of *Led Zeppelin* and is considered one of the most influential guitarists of all time.

Example 5.25

Lee Kuan Yew, Singaporean Prime Minister 1965 to 1990, September 16, 1923, 09:07 hours

Hour	Day	Month	Year
乙	壬	辛	癸
Yin Wood	**Yang Water**	Yin Metal	Yin Water
巳	辰	酉	亥
Snake	Dragon	Rooster	Pig
庚 **Yang Metal**			

Lee is a Yang Water Day Stem. The Hurting Officer Yin Wood is present in the Hour. It sits on a Snake Branch, which contains Yang Metal, the Resource for the Yang Water Day Stem. Lee was the Prime Minister of Singapore from 1959 (Yin Earth Pig year) to 1990 (Yang Metal Horse year).

Example 5.26

Jose Feliciano, Puerto Rican Singer and Musician, September 10, 1945, 10:00 hours

Hour	Day	Month	Year
乙	壬	乙	乙
Yin Wood	**Yang Water**	**Yin Wood**	**Yin Wood**
巳	午	酉	酉
Snake	Horse	**Rooster**	**Rooster**
庚 **Yang Metal**		辛 **Yin Metal**	辛 **Yin Metal**

Feliciano is a Yang Water Day Stem. The Hurting Officer Yin Wood is present in the Year, Month and Hour. In the Year and Month, it sits on a Rooster Branch, which contains Yin Metal, the Resource for the Yang Water Day Stem. In the Hour, it sits on a Snake Branch, which contains Yang Metal, the Resource for the Yang Water day Stem. Feliciano is known for his hits *Light My Fire* and *Feliz Navidad*.

Example 5.27

Debbie Gibson, American Singer and Actress, August 31, 1970, 02:57 hours

Hour	Day	Month	Year
癸	癸	甲	庚
Yin Water	**Yin Water**	**Yang Wood**	Yang Metal
丑	未	申	戌
Ox	Sheep	**Monkey**	Dog
		庚 **Yang Metal**	

Gibson is a Yin Water Day Stem. The Hurting Officer Yang Wood is present in the Month. It sits on a Monkey Branch, which contains Yang Metal, the Resource for the Yin Water Day Stem. Gibson is the youngest female artist to write, produce and perform a US Number One Single with *Foolish Beat* in 1988 (Yang Earth Dragon year).

Example 5.28

Matthew McConaughey, American Actor, November 4, 1969, 19:34 hours

Hour	Day	Month	Year
壬	癸	甲	己
Yang Water	**Yin Water**	**Yang Wood**	Yin Earth
戌	未	戌	酉
Dog	Sheep	**Dog**	Rooster
		辛 **Yin Metal**	

McConaughey is a Yin Water Day Stem. The Hurting Officer Yang Wood is present in the Month. It sits on a Dog Branch, which contains Yin Metal, the Resource for the Yin Water Day Stem. He won a Best Actor Oscar for the *Dallas Buyers Club* in 2014 (Yang Wood Horse year).

Days Sitting on the Hurting Officer

When the Hurting Officer is present in the Day Branch, there may be challenges with the marriage for women. The Hurting Officer attacks the Power element, which represents the Spouse element for women.

Table 5.3 lists the 12 Days that Sit on the Hurting Officer

Table 5.3: Days Sitting on the Hurting Officer

甲 Yang Wood	甲 Yang Wood	乙 Yin Wood	丙 Yang Fire	丁 Yin Fire	戊 Yang Earth
午 Horse	戌 Dog	巳 Snake	午 Horse	巳 Snake	戌 Dog
己 Yin Earth	庚 Yang Metal	庚 Yang Metal	辛 Yin Metal	壬 Yang Water	癸 Yin Water
巳 Snake	子 Rat	辰 Dragon	亥 Pig	辰 Dragon	亥 Pig

Example 5.29

Stephanie Seymour, American Model and Actress,
July 23, 1968, 07:43 hours DST

Hour	Day	Month	Year
丁	甲	己	戊
Yin Fire	**Yang Wood**	Yin Earth	Yang Earth
卯	午	未	申
Rabbit	**Horse**	Sheep	Monkey
	丁 **Yin Fire**		

Seymour is a Yang Wood Day Stem. The Hurting Officer Yin Fire is hidden in the Horse Day Branch. Seymour has been married twice. From 1989 (Yin Earth Snake year) to 1990 (Yang Metal Horse year), she was married to Tommy Andrews. In 1995 (Yin Wood Pig year), Seymour married publisher Peter Brant.

Example 5.30

Sarah Brightman, English Singer and Actress,
August 14, 1960, 05:45 hours DST

Hour	Day	Month	Year
丙	甲	甲	庚
Yang Fire	**Yang Wood**	Yang Wood	Yang Metal
寅	戌	申	子
Tiger	**Dog**	Monkey	Rat
	丁 **Yin Fire**		

Brightman is a Yang Wood Day Stem. The Hurting Officer Yin Fire is hidden in the Dog Day Branch. She has been married and divorced twice. From 1979 (Yin Earth Sheep year) to 1983 (Yin Water Pig year), Brightman was married to Andrew Graham-Stewart, the manager of the German band *Tangerine Dream*. From 1984 (Yang Wood Rat year) to 1990 (Yang Metal Horse year), she was married to music composer Andrew Lloyd Webber. Brightman was also in a ten-year relationship with Frank Peterson.

Example 5.31

Halle Berry, American Actress, August 14, 1966, 23:59 hours DST

Hour	Day	Month	Year
丁	乙	乙	丙
Yin Fire	**Yin Wood**	Yin Wood	Yang Fire
亥	巳	未	午
Pig	**Snake**	Sheep	Horse
	丙 **Yang Fire**		

Berry is a Yin Wood Day Stem. The Hurting Officer Yang Fire is hidden in the Snake Day Branch. She has been married and divorced three times. From January 1, 1993 (still Yang Water Monkey year) to 1997 (Yin Fire Ox year), Berry was married to baseball player David Justice. From January 2001 (still Yang Metal Dragon year) to January 2005 (still Yang Wood Monkey year), she was married to singer-songwriter Eric Benet. From 2005 (Yin Wood Rooster year) to 2010 (Yang Metal Tiger year), Berry had a relationship with model Gabriel Aubry, with whom she has a daughter. From 2013 (Yin Water Snake year) to 2016 (Yang Fire Monkey year), Berry was married to actor Olivier Martinez, with whom she has a son.

Example 5.32

Kathleen Turner, American Actress,
June 19, 1954, 19:40 hours

Hour	Day	Month	Year
戊	丙	庚	甲
Yang Earth	**Yang Fire**	Yang Metal	Yang Wood
戌	午	午	午
Dog	Horse	Horse	Horse
	己 **Yin Earth**		

Turner is a Yang Fire Day Stem. The Hurting Officer Yin Earth is hidden in the Horse Day Branch. From 1984 (Yang Wood Rat year) to 2007 (Yin Fire Pig year), Turner was married to real estate entrepreneur Jay Weiss, with whom she has a daughter.

Example 5.33

Jennifer Aniston, American Actress,
February 11, 1969, 22:22 hours

Hour	Day	Month	Year
辛	丁	乙	戊
Yin Metal	**Yin Fire**	Yin Wood	Yang Earth
亥	巳	丑	申
Pig	Snake	Ox	Monkey
	戊 **Yang Earth**		

Aniston is a Yin Fire Day Stem. The Hurting Officer Yang Earth is hidden in the Snake Day Branch. Aniston has been married twice. From 2000 (Yang Metal Dragon year) to 2005 (Yin Wood Rooster year), she was married to actor Brad Pitt. From 2015 (Yin Wood Sheep year) to 2017 (Yin Fire Rooster year), Aniston was married to actor Justin Theroux.

Example 5.34

Lucy Lawless, New Zealand Actress, March 29, 1968, 06:25 hours

Hour	Day	Month	Year
乙	戊	丙	戊
Yin Wood	**Yang Earth**	Yang Fire	Yang Earth
卯	戌	辰	申
Rabbit	**Dog**	Dragon	Monkey
	辛 **Yin Metal**		

Lawless is a Yang Earth Day Stem. The Hurting Officer Yin Metal is hidden in the Dog Day Branch. Lawless has been married twice. From 1988 (Yang Earth Dragon year) to 1995 (Yin Wood Pig year), she was married to Garth Lawless. In 1998 (Yang Earth Tiger year), Lawless married producer Rob Tapert.

Example 5.35

Gloria Vanderbilt, American Heiress and Fashion Designer, February 20, 1924, 09:55 hours

Hour	Day	Month	Year
己	己	丙	甲
Yin Earth	**Yin Earth**	Yang Fire	Yang Wood
巳	巳	寅	子
Snake	**Snake**	Tiger	Rat
	庚 Yang Metal		

Vanderbilt is a Yin Earth Day Stem. The Hurting Officer Yang Metal is hidden in the Snake Day Branch. Vanderbilt was married four times. From 1941 (Yin Metal Snake year) to 1945 (Yin Wood Rooster year), she was the second wife of agent Pat DiCicco. From 1945 (Yin Wood Rooster year), Vanderbilt was the third and last wife of conductor Leopold Stokowski, 42 years her senior. She was then the second of four wives of director Sidney Lumet, from 1956 (Yang Fire Monkey year) to 1963 (Yin Water Rabbit year). Her fourth and final marriage was to author Wyatt Emory Cooper from 1963 (Yin Water Rabbit year) to January 1978 (Still Yin Fire Snake year), ending with his death.

Example 5.36

Jennifer Lopez, American Actress and Singer, July 24, 1969, 05:49 hours DST

Hour	Day	Month	Year
戊	庚	辛	己
Yang Earth	**Yang Metal**	Yin Metal	Yin Earth
寅	子	未	酉
Tiger	**Rat**	Sheep	Rooster
	癸 Yin Water		

Lopez is a Yang Metal Day Stem. The Hurting Officer Yin Water is hidden in the Rat Day Branch. Lopez has been married and divorced three times. From February 1997 to January 1998 (still Yin Fire Ox year), she was married to Cuban waiter Ojani Noa. From September 2001 (Yin Metal Snake year) to June 2002 (Yang Water Horse year), Lopez was married to dancer Cris Judd. From 2004 (Yang Wood Monkey year) to 2014 (Yang Wood Horse year), she was married to singer Marc Anthony, with whom she had two children.

Example 5.37

Christina Onassis, Greek Businesswoman,
December 11, 1950, 15:00 hours

Hour	Day	Month	Year
甲	庚	戊	庚
Yang Wood	**Yang Metal**	Yang Earth	Yang Metal
申	辰	子	寅
Monkey	**Dragon**	Rat	Tiger
	癸 **Yin Water**		

Onassis is a Yang Metal Day Stem. The Hurting Officer Yin Water is hidden in the Dragon Day Branch. Onassis was married and divorced four times. In 1971 (Yin Metal Pig year), she was married for nine months to real estate developer Joseph Bolker. Her second husband was banking and shipping heir Alexander Andreadis, to whom she was married from 1975 (Yin Wood Rabbit year) to 1977 (Yin Fire Snake year). Onassis's third husband was Russian shipping agent Sergei Kauzov from 1978 (Yang Earth Horse year) to 1980 (Yang Metal Monkey year). Her fourth and final marriage was to French businessman Thierry Roussel from 1984 (Yang Wood Rat year) to 1987 (Yin Fire Rabbit year), with whom she shared daughter Athina.

Example 5.38

Raquel Welch, American Actress,
September 5, 1940, 14:04 hours

Hour	Day	Month	Year
乙	辛	乙	庚
Yin Wood	**Yin Metal**	Yin Wood	Yang Metal
未	亥	酉	辰
Sheep	**Pig**	Rooster	Dragon
	壬 **Yang Water**		

Welch is a Yin Metal Day Stem. The Hurting Officer Yang Water is hidden in the Pig Day Branch. Welch has been married and divorced four times. From 1959 (Yin Earth Pig year) to 1964 (Yang Wood Dragon year), she was married to high school sweetheart James Welch. From 1967 (Yin Fire Sheep year) to 1972 (Yang Water Rat year), she was married to producer Patrick Curtis. Her third husband was producer Andre Weinfeld from 1980 (Yang Metal Monkey year) to 1990 (Yang Metal Horse year). From 1999 (Yin Earth Rabbit year) to 2004 (Yang Wood Monkey year), Welch was married to pizzeria owner Richard Palmer.

Example 5.39

Khloe Kardashian, American Media Personality,
June 27, 1984, 22:55 hours

Hour	Day	Month	Year
辛	壬	庚	甲
Yin Metal	**Yang Water**	Yang Metal	Yang Wood
亥	辰	午	子
Pig	**Dragon**	Horse	Rat
	乙 **Yin Wood**		

Kardashian is a Yang Water Day Stem. The Hurting Officer Yin Wood is hidden in the Dragon Day Branch. Kardashian was married to basketball player Lamar Odom from 2009 (Yin Earth Ox year) to 2016 (Yang Fire Monkey year). From 2016 (Yang Fire Monkey year) to 2021 (Yin Metal Ox year), she had a relationship with basketball player Tristan Thompson, with whom she has daughter True.

Example 5.40

Kate Beckinsale, English Actress and Model, July 26, 1973

Hour	Day	Month	Year
	癸	己	癸
	Yin Water	Yin Earth	Yin Water
	亥	未	丑
	Pig	Sheep	Ox
	甲 **Yang Wood**		

Beckinsale is a Yin Water Day Stem. The Hurting Officer Yang Wood is hidden in the Pig Day Branch. From 1995 (Yin Wood Pig year) to 2003 (Yin Water Sheep year), Beckinsale was in a relationship with actor Michael Sheen. From 2004 (Yang Wood Monkey year) to 2019 (Yin Earth Pig year), she was married to director Len Wiseman.

Summary

In summary, what to look for in a chart with regard to the Hurting Officer:

1. Hurting Officer Sitting on the Resource Pillar.
2. Days Sitting on the Hurting Officer.

陸

Chapter Six

Chapter Six Wealth

The Wealth element is the element that is controlled by the Day Stem. For example, for a Fire Day Stem, the Wealth element is Metal as Fire controls Metal. For a Water Day Stem, the Wealth element is Fire as Water controls Fire.

Table 6.1 indicates the Day Stem and the corresponding Direct Wealth (opposite polarity) and Indirect Wealth (same polarity).

Table 6.1 Day Stem with Direct Wealth and Indirect Wealth

Day Stem	Direct Wealth	Indirect Wealth
甲 Yang Wood	己 Yin Earth	戊 Yang Earth
乙 Yin Wood	戊 Yang Earth	己 Yin Earth
丙 Yang Fire	辛 Yin Metal	庚 Yang Metal
丁 Yin Fire	庚 Yang Metal	辛 Yin Metal
戊 Yang Earth	癸 Yin Water	壬 Yang Water
己 Yin Earth	壬 Yang Water	癸 Yin Water
庚 Yang Metal	乙 Yin Wood	甲 Yang Wood
辛 Yin Metal	甲 Yang Wood	乙 Yin Wood
壬 Yang Water	丁 Yin Fire	丙 Yang Fire
癸 Yin Water	丙 Yang Fire	丁 Yin Fire

Direct Wealth is income that is earned, while Indirect Wealth consists of gifts, inheritances, investments and income from undefined sources, which may include gambling. In modern times, it is no longer necessary to differentiate between the two types of Wealth.

When the Wealth element is present in the Stems, there is generosity in assisting others. There is also the potential for Rivals to seize them. The more Wealth Stems there are, the more competition there is for it.

When the Wealth element is hidden in the Branches, there is no competition for it.

Wealth hidden in the Branches

The following examples illustrate examples of the Wealth element hidden in the Branches for all Day Stems. The Wealth element in the branches is indicated in bold.

Example 6.1

Kristen Stewart, American Actress, April 9, 1990, 09:21 hours DST

Hour	Day	Month	Year
戊	甲	庚	庚
Yang Earth	**Yang Wood**	Yang Metal	Yang Metal
辰	辰	辰	午
Dragon	**Dragon**	**Dragon**	**Horse**
戊 **Yang Earth**	戊 **Yang Earth**	戊 **Yang Earth**	己 **Yin Earth**

Stewart is a Yang Wood Day Stem. The Wealth element Earth is hidden in the Dragon Month, Day and Hour Branches, as well as the Horse Year Branch. There is also Wealth present in the Hour Stem. Stewart's net worth is USD 70 million.

Example 6.2

Madonna, American Singer and Actress, August 16, 1958, 07:05 hours

Hour	Day	Month	Year
庚	乙	庚	戊
Yang Metal	**Yin Wood**	Yang Metal	Yang Earth
辰	丑	申	戌
Dragon	**Ox**	**Monkey**	**Dog**
戊 Yang Earth	己 Yin Earth	戊 Yang Earth	戊 Yang Earth

Madonna is a Yin Wood Day Stem. The Wealth element Earth is hidden in the Dog Year Branch, Monkey Month Branch, Ox Day Branch and Dragon Hour Branch. It is also present in the Year Stem. Madonna's net worth is USD 570 million.

Example 6.3

Mae West, American Actress and Singer, August 17, 1893, 22:30 hours

Hour	Day	Month	Year
己	丙	庚	癸
Yin Earth	**Yang Fire**	Yang Metal	Yin Water
亥	戌	申	巳
Pig	**Dog**	**Monkey**	**Snake**
	辛 Yin Metal	庚 Yang Metal	庚 Yang Metal

West is a Yang Fire Day Stem. The Wealth element Metal is hidden in the Snake Year Branch, Monkey Month Branch and Dog Day Branch. There is also Wealth present in the Month Stem. At the time of her death in 1980 (Yang Metal Monkey year), West's estate was worth USD one million.

Example 6.4

Simon Le Bon, English Singer and Musician *Duran Duran*, October 27, 1958, 21:00 hours

Hour	Day	Month	Year
辛	丁	壬	戊
Yin Metal	**Yin Fire**	Yang Water	Yang Earth
亥	丑	戌	戌
Pig	Ox	Dog	Dog
	辛 **Yin Metal**	辛 **Yin Metal**	辛 **Yin Metal**

Le Bon is a Yin Fire Day Stem. The Wealth element Metal is hidden in the Dog Year and Month Branches and Ox Day Branch. It is also present in the Hour Stem. Le Bon has a net worth of USD 65 million.

Example 6.5

Athina Onassis, Athina Onassis French-Greek Heiress and Equestrian, January 29, 1985, 02:50 hours

Hour	Day	Month	Year
癸	戊	丁	甲
Yin Water	**Yang Earth**	Yin Fire	Yang Wood
丑	辰	丑	子
Ox	Dragon	Ox	Rat
癸 **Yin Water**	癸 **Yin Water**	癸 **Yin Water**	癸 **Yin Water**

Onassis is a Yang Earth Day Stem. The Wealth element Water is hidden in the Rat Year Branch, Dragon Day Branch and Ox Month and Hour Branches. It is also present in the Hour Stem. Her net worth is around USD one billion.

Example 6.6

George Clooney, American Actor and Filmmaker, May 6, 1961, 02:58 hours

Hour	Day	Month	Year
乙	己	壬	辛
Yin Wood	**Yin Earth**	Yang Water	Yin Metal
丑	亥	辰	丑
Ox	**Pig**	**Dragon**	**Ox**
癸 Yin Water	壬 Yang Water	癸 Yin Water	癸 Yin Water

Clooney is a Yin Earth Day Stem. The Wealth element Water is hidden in the Ox Year and Hour Branches, Dragon Month Branch and Pig Day Branch. It is also present in the Month Stem. Clooney is worth USD 500 million.

Example 6.7

Melanie Laurent, French Actress, February 21, 1983, 14:00 hours

Hour	Day	Month	Year
癸	庚	甲	癸
Yin Water	**Yang Metal**	Yang Wood	Yin Water
未	辰	寅	亥
Sheep	**Dragon**	**Tiger**	**Pig**
乙 Yin Wood	乙 Yin Wood	甲 Yang Wood	甲 Yang Wood

Laurent is a Yang Metal Day Stem. The Wealth element Wood is hidden in the Pig Year Branch, Tiger Month Branch, Dragon Day Branch and Sheep Hour Branch. It is also present in the Month Stem. Laurent is worth USD eight million.

Example 6.8

Michael Jordan, American Basketball Player, February 17, 1963, 13:40 hours

Hour	Day	Month	Year
乙	辛	甲	癸
Yin Wood	**Yin Metal**	Yang Wood	Yin Water
未	卯	寅	卯
Sheep	**Rabbit**	**Tiger**	**Rabbit**
乙 Yin Wood	乙 Yin Wood	甲 Yang Wood	乙 Yin Wood

Jordan is a Yin Metal Day Stem. The Wealth element Wood is hidden in the Rabbit Year and Day Branches, the Tiger Month Branch and the Sheep Hour Branch. It is also present in the Month Stem and Hour Stem. Jordan is worth USD 2.1 billion.

Example 6.9

Tom Cruise, American Actor, July 3, 1962, 15:06 hours DST

Hour	Day	Month	Year
丁	壬	丁	壬
Yin Fire	**Yang Water**	Yin Fire	Yang Water
未	寅	未	寅
Sheep	**Tiger**	**Sheep**	**Tiger**
丁 Yin Fire	丙 Yang Fire	丁 Yin Fire	丙 Yang Fire

Cruise is a Yang Water Day Stem. The Wealth element Fire is hidden in the Tiger Year and Day Branches and the Sheep Month and Hour Branches. It is also present in the Month and Hour Stems. Cruise is worth USD 600 million.

Example 6.10

Vin Diesel, American Actor,
July 18, 1967, 15:35 hours DST

Hour	Day	Month	Year
己	癸	丁	丁
Yin Earth	**Yin Water**	Yin Fire	Yin Fire
未	未	未	未
Sheep	**Sheep**	**Sheep**	**Sheep**
丁 Yin Fire	丁 Yin Fire	丁 Yin Fire	丁 Yin Fire

Diesel is a Yin Water Day Stem. The Wealth element Fire is hidden in the Sheep Year, Month, Day and Hour Branches. It is also present in the Month and Year Stems. Diesel is worth USD 225 million.

The Five Yang Stem Combinations with Wealth

The Five Yang Stems combine with the Wealth element as shown in Table 6.2.

Table 6.2 Yang Day Stem Combining with the Wealth element

Yang Day Stem	Wealth element Stem
甲 Yang Wood	己 Yin Earth
丙 Yang Fire	辛 Yin Metal
戊 Yang Earth	癸 Yin Water
庚 Yang Metal	乙 Yin Wood
壬 Yang Water	丁 Yin Fire

The following examples illustrate each Yang Stem combining with the Wealth element within the chart. The Stems have to be adjacent to each other for the Wealth Combination to occur and have to involve the Day Stem. The Wealth Stem can be present in the Month or Hour Pillar. The Wealth Combinations are in bold.

Example 6.11

Lisa Kudrow, American Actress, July 30, 1963, 04:37 hours

Hour	Day	Month	Year
丙	甲	己	癸
Yang Fire	**Yang Wood**	**Yin Earth**	Yin Water
寅	戌	未	卯
Tiger	Dog	Sheep	Rabbit
戊 Yang Earth	戊 Yang Earth	己 Yin Earth	

Kudrow is a Yang Wood Day Stem. It combines with the Yin Earth Month Stem. The Wealth element Earth is also hidden in the Sheep Month Branch, Dog Day Branch and Tiger Hour Branch. Kudrow is worth USD 130 million.

Example 6.12

Gabriela Sabatini, Argentine Tennis Player, May 16, 1970, 06:30 hours

Hour	Day	Month	Year
辛	丙	辛	庚
Yin Metal	**Yang Fire**	**Yin Metal**	Yang Metal
卯	申	巳	戌
Rabbit	Monkey	Snake	Dog
	庚 Yang Metal	庚 Yang Metal	辛 Yin Metal

Sabatini is a Yang Fire Day Stem. It combines with the Yin Metal Stem in the Month and Hour Pillars. There is also a Yang Metal Year Stem. The Wealth element Metal is also hidden in the Dog Year Branch, Snake Month Branch and Monkey Day Branch. Sabatini is worth USD eight million.

Example 6.13

Steve Wozniak, American Electronics Engineer,
August 11, 1950, 09:45 hours DST

Hour	Day	Month	Year
丙	戊	癸	庚
Yang Fire	**Yang Earth**	**Yin Water**	Yang Metal
辰	寅	未	寅
Dragon	Tiger	Sheep	Tiger
癸 Yin Water			

Wozniak is a Yang Earth Day Stem. It combines with the Yin Water Month Stem. The Wealth element Water is also hidden in the Dragon Hour Branch. Wozniak is worth USD 100 million.

Example 6.14

Sultan Hassanal Bolkiah, Bruneian Royalty,
July 15, 1946, 12:00 hours

Hour	Day	Month	Year
壬	庚	乙	丙
Yang Water	**Yang Metal**	**Yin Wood**	Yang Fire
午	寅	未	戌
Horse	Tiger	Sheep	Dog
	甲 Yang Wood	乙 Yin Wood	

The Sultan is a Yang Metal Day Stem. It combines with the Yin Wood Month Stem. The Wealth element Wood is also hidden in the Sheep Month Branch and Tiger Day Branch. The Sultan is worth USD 28 billion.

Example 6.15

Freddie Mercury, British Singer *Queen*,
September 5, 1946, 06:30 hours

Hour	Day	Month	Year
癸	壬	丁	丙
Yin Water	**Yang Water**	**Yin Fire**	Yang Fire
卯	午	酉	戌
Rabbit	Horse	Rooster	Dog
	丁 Yin Fire		丁 Yin Fire

Mercury is a Yang Water Day Stem. It combines with the Yin Fire Month Stem. The Wealth element Fire is also present in the Year Stem. It is also hidden in the Dog Year Branch and the Horse Day Branch. At the time of his death in 1991 (Yin Metal Sheep year), his net worth was USD 50 million.

Indirect Wealth in the Month or Hour Stem

When the Indirect Wealth (same polarity) is present in the Month or Hour Stem, there is significant wealth.

The following examples illustrate the Indirect Wealth present in the Month or Hour for all Day Stems. The Indirect Wealth in the Stems is in bold.

Example 6.16

Kylie Jenner, American Media Personality, August 10, 1997, 17:25 hours DST

Hour	Day	Month	Year
壬	甲	戊	丁
Yang Water	**Yang Wood**	**Yang Earth**	Yin Fire
申	申	申	丑
Monkey	Monkey	Monkey	Ox
戊 Yang Earth	戊 Yang Earth	戊 Yang Earth	己 Yin Earth

Jenner is a Yang Wood Day Stem. The Indirect Wealth Yang Earth is present in the Month Stem. The Wealth element Earth is also hidden in the Ox Year Branch and the Monkey Month, Day and Hour Branches. Jenner is worth USD 700 million.

Example 6.17

Frankie Valli, American Singer *The Four Seasons*, May 3, 1934, 09:00 hours DST

Hour	Day	Month	Year
戊	甲	戊	甲
Yang Earth	**Yang Wood**	**Yang Earth**	Yang Wood
辰	戌	辰	戌
Dragon	Dog	Dragon	Dog
戊 Yang Earth	戊 Yang Earth	戊 Yang Earth	戊 Yang Earth

Valli is a Yang Wood Day Stem. The Indirect Wealth Yang Earth is present in the Month and Hour Stems. The Wealth element Earth is also hidden in the Dog Year and Day Branches and the Dragon Month and Hour Branches. Valli is worth USD 70 million.

Example 6.18

Gary Barlow, English Singer-Songwriter *Take That*,
January 20, 1971, 12:20 hours

Hour	Day	Month	Year
壬	乙	己	庚
Yang Water	**Yin Wood**	**Yin Earth**	Yang Metal
午	巳	丑	戌
Horse	Snake	Ox	Dog
己 Yin Earth	戊 Yang Earth	己 Yin Earth	戊 Yang Earth

Barlow is a Yin Wood Day Stem. The Indirect Wealth Yin Earth is present in the Month Stem. The Wealth element Earth is also hidden in the Dog Year Branch, Ox Month Branch, Snake Day Branch and Horse Hour Branch. Barlow is worth USD 105 million.

Example 6.19

Liz Hurley, English Actress and Model,
June 10, 1965, 06:40 hours

Hour	Day	Month	Year
己	乙	壬	乙
Yin Earth	**Yin Wood**	Yang Water	Yin Wood
卯	未	午	巳
Rabbit	Sheep	Horse	Snake
	己 Yin Earth	己 Yin Earth	戊 Yang Earth

Hurley is a Yin Wood Day Stem. The Indirect Wealth Yin Earth is present in the Hour Stem. The Wealth element Earth is also hidden in the Snake Year Branch, Horse Month Branch and the Sheep Day Branch. Hurley is worth USD 50 million.

Example 6.20

Paris Hilton, American Media Personality,
February 17, 1981, 02:30 hours

Hour	Day	Month	Year
己	丙	庚	辛
Yin Earth	**Yang Fire**	**Yang Metal**	Yin Metal
丑	寅	寅	酉
Ox	Tiger	Tiger	Rooster
辛 Yin Metal			辛 Yin Metal

Hilton is a Yang Fire Day Stem. The Indirect Wealth Yang Metal is present in the Month Stem. The Direct Wealth Yin Metal is present in the Year Stem. The Wealth element Metal is also hidden in the Rooster Year Branch and the Ox Hour Branch. Hilton is worth USD 300 million.

Example 6.21

Pamela Anderson, Canadian-American Actress and Model,
July 1, 1967, 04:08 hours

Hour	Day	Month	Year
庚	丙	丙	丁
Yang Metal	**Yang Fire**	Yang Fire	Yin Fire
寅	寅	午	未
Tiger	Tiger	Horse	Sheep

Anderson is a Yang Fire Day Stem. The Indirect Wealth Yang Metal is present in the Hour Stem. Anderson is worth USD 20 million.

Example 6.22

Jeremy Irons, English Actor,
September 19, 1948, 02:00 hours

Hour	Day	Month	Year
辛	丁	辛	戊
Yin Metal	**Yin Fire**	**Yin Metal**	Yang Earth
丑	未	酉	子
Ox	Sheep	Rooster	Rat
辛 Yin Metal		辛 Yin Metal	

Irons is a Yin Fire Day Stem. The Indirect Wealth Yin Metal is present in the Month and Hour Stems. The Wealth element is also hidden in the Rooster Month Branch and Ox Hour Branch. Irons is worth USD 25 million.

Example 6.23

Tina Turner, American-Swiss Singer and Actress,
November 26, 1939, 22:10 hours

Hour	Day	Month	Year
辛	丁	乙	己
Yin Metal	**Yin Fire**	Yin Wood	Yin Earth
亥	卯	亥	卯
Pig	Rabbit	Pig	Rabbit

Turner is a Yin Fire Day Stem. The Indirect Wealth Yin Metal is present in the Hour Stem. Turner is worth USD 250 million.

Example 6.24

Paul Theroux, American Writer and Novelist, April 10, 1941, 19:00 hours

Hour	Day	Month	Year
壬	戊	壬	辛
Yang Water	**Yang Earth**	**Yang Water**	Yin Metal
戌	子	辰	巳
Dog	Rat	Dragon	Snake
	癸 Yin Water	癸 Yin Water	

Theroux is a Yang Earth Day Stem. The Indirect Wealth Yang Water is present in the Month and Hour Stems. The Wealth element Water is also hidden in the Dragon Month Branch and Rat Day Branch. Theroux is worth USD 10 million.

Example 6.25

Denzel Washington, American Actor and Director, December 28, 1954, 00:09 hours

Hour	Day	Month	Year
壬	戊	丁	甲
Yang Water	**Yang Earth**	Yin Fire	Yang Wood
子	午	丑	午
Rat	Horse	Ox	Horse
癸 Yin Water		癸 Yin Water	

Washington is a Yang Earth Day Stem. The Indirect Wealth Yang Water is present in the Hour Stem. The Wealth element Water is also hidden in the Ox Month Branch and the Rat Hour Branch.

Example 6.26

Charlotte Casiraghi, Monegasque Royalty,
August 3, 1986, 19:00 hours DST

Hour	Day	Month	Year
癸	己	乙	丙
Yin Water	**Yin Earth**	Yin Wood	Yang Fire
酉	卯	未	寅
Rooster	Rabbit	Sheep	Tiger

Charlotte is a Yin Earth Day Stem. The Indirect Wealth Yin Water is present in the Hour Stem. Charlotte is worth USD 30 million.

Example 6.27

Kesha, American Singer-Songwriter,
March 1, 1987, 00:34 hours

Hour	Day	Month	Year
甲	己	癸	丁
Yang Wood	**Yin Earth**	**Yin Water**	Yin Fire
子	酉	卯	卯
Rat	Rooster	Rabbit	Rabbit
癸 Yin Water			

Kesha is a Yin Earth Day Stem. The Indirect Wealth Yin Water is present in the Month Stem. The Wealth element Water is also hidden in the Rat Hour Branch. Kesha is worth USD five million.

Example 6.28

Ashton Kutcher, American Actor and Entrepreneur, February 7, 1978, 12:30 hours

Hour	Day	Month	Year
壬	庚	甲	戊
Yang Water	**Yang Metal**	**Yang Wood**	Yang Earth
午	子	寅	午
Horse	Rat	Tiger	Horse
		甲 Yang Wood	

Kutcher is a Yang Metal Day Stem. The Indirect Wealth Yang Wood is present in the Month Stem. The Wealth element Wood is also hidden in the Tiger Month Branch. Kutcher is worth USD 200 million.

Example 6.29

Adrien Brody, American Actor and Producer, April 14, 1973, 15:30 hours

Hour	Day	Month	Year
甲	庚	丙	癸
Yang Wood	**Yang Metal**	Yang Fire	Yin Water
申	辰	辰	丑
Monkey	Dragon	Dragon	Ox
	乙 Yin Wood	乙 Yin Wood	

Brody is a Yang Metal Day Stem. The Indirect Wealth Yang Wood is present in the Hour Stem. The Wealth element Wood is also hidden in the Dragon Month and Day Branches. Brody is worth USD 10 million.

Example 6.30

Novak Djokovic, Serbian Tennis Player,
May 22, 1987, 23:25 hours DST

Hour	Day	Month	Year
己	辛	乙	丁
Yin Earth	**Yin Metal**	**Yin Wood**	Yin Fire
亥	未	巳	卯
Pig	Sheep	Snake	Rabbit
甲 Yang Wood	乙 Yin Wood		乙 Yin Wood

Djokovic is a Yin Metal Day Stem. The Indirect Wealth Yin Wood is present in the Month Stem. The Wealth element Wood is also hidden in the Rabbit Year Branch, Sheep Day Branch and Pig Hour Branch. Djokovic is worth USD 220 million.

Example 6.31

Conan O'Brien, American Television Host and Comedian,
April 18, 1963, 13:48 hours

Hour	Day	Month	Year
乙	辛	丙	癸
Yin Wood	**Yin Metal**	Yang Fire	Yin Water
未	卯	辰	卯
Sheep	Rabbit	Dragon	Rabbit
乙 Yin Wood	乙 Yin Wood	乙 Yin Wood	乙 Yin Wood

O'Brien is a Yin Metal Day Stem. The Indirect Wealth Yin Wood is present in the Hour Stem. The Wealth element Wood is also hidden in the Rabbit Year and Day Branches, Dragon Month Branch and Sheep Hour Branch. O'Brien is worth USD 200 million.

Example 6.32

Robert Redford, American Actor and Director,
August 18, 1936, 20:02 hours

Hour	Day	Month	Year
庚	壬	丙	丙
Yang Metal	**Yang Water**	**Yang Fire**	Yang Fire
戌	申	申	子
Dog	Monkey	Monkey	Rat
丁 Yin Fire			

Redford is a Yang Water Day Stem. The Indirect Wealth Yang Fire is present in the Month Stem. It is also present in the Year Stem. The Wealth element Fire is also hidden in the Dog Hour Branch. Redford is worth USD 200 million.

Example 6.33

Benedict Cumberbatch, English Actor,
July 19, 1976, 12:00 hours

Hour	Day	Month	Year
丙	壬	乙	丙
Yang Fire	**Yang Water**	Yin Wood	Yang Fire
午	申	未	辰
Horse	Monkey	Sheep	Dragon
丁 Yin Fire		丁 Yin Fire	

Cumberbatch is a Yang Water Day Stem. The Indirect Wealth Yang Fire is present in the Hour Stem. It is also present in the Year Stem. The Wealth element Fire is also hidden in the Sheep Month Branch and Horse Hour Branch. Cumberbatch is worth USD 40 million.

Example 6.34

Kaley Cuoco, American Actress,
November 30, 1985, 12:18 hours

Hour	Day	Month	Year
戊	癸	丁	乙
Yang Earth	**Yin Water**	**Yin Fire**	Yin Wood
午	酉	亥	丑
Horse	Rooster	Pig	Ox
丁 Yin Fire			

Cuoco is a Yin Water Day Stem. The Indirect Wealth Yin Fire is present in the Month Stem. The Wealth element Fire is also hidden in the Horse Hour Branch. Cuoco is worth USD 100 million.

Example 6.35

Sir Michael Palin, English Comedian, Actor and Television Presenter, May 5, 1943, 11:45 hours DST

Hour	Day	Month	Year
丁	癸	丁	癸
Yin Fire	**Yin Water**	**Yin Fire**	Yin Water
巳	亥	巳	未
Snake	Pig	Snake	Sheep
丙 Yang Fire		丙 Yang Fire	丁 Yin Fire

Palin is a Yin Water Day Stem. The Indirect Wealth Yin Fire is present in the Month and Hour Stems. The Wealth element Fire is also hidden in the Sheep Year Branch and the Snake Month and Hour Branches. Palin is worth USD 25 million.

Summary

In summary, what to look for in a chart with regard to the Wealth:

1. Wealth hidden in the Branches.
2. Yang Stem Combinations with Wealth.
3. Indirect Wealth in the Month or Hour Stem.

Chapter Seven

Chapter Seven Resource

The Resource element is the one that gives birth to the Day Stem. Those who use the Resource element enjoy very good lives, as their wealth may be inherited or derived from opportunities. Table 7.1 indicates the Day Stem and corresponding Direct Resource (Opposite Polarity) and Indirect Resource (Same Polarity).

Table 7.1 Day Stem and Direct and Indirect Resource

Day Stem	Direct Resource	Indirect Resource
甲 Yang Wood	癸 Yin Water	壬 Yang Water
乙 Yin Wood	壬 Yang Water	癸 Yin Water
丙 Yang Fire	乙 Yin Wood	甲 Yang Wood
丁 Yin Fire	甲 Yang Wood	乙 Yin Wood
戊 Yang Earth	丁 Yin Fire	丙 Yang Fire
己 Yin Earth	丙 Yang Fire	丁 Yin Fire
庚 Yang Metal	己 Yin Earth	戊 Yang Earth
辛 Yin Metal	戊 Yang Earth	己 Yin Earth
壬 Yang Water	辛 Yin Metal	庚 Yang Metal
癸 Yin Water	庚 Yang Metal	辛 Yin Metal

There is no distinction between Direct Resource and Indirect Resource. The Resource element indicates fame, support and a caring mother. Those with a prominent Resource element are kind and wise, enjoy solitude and relate well to the mother.

Resource Sitting on the Birth Pillar

When the Resource is sitting on the Birth Life Stage (as determined by the Three Harmony Life Stages), then there is professional recognition and success. There are five Yang Resource Stems and five Yin Resource Stems to consider.

Table 7.2 lists the 12 Life Stages for the Yang Resource Stems. The Life Stage to take into account is the Birth, which has been highlighted. Note that Yang Wood and Yang Metal cannot sit on the Birth Branch as they are of the opposite polarity.

Table 7.2 12 Life Stages for the Yang Resource Stems

Stem Life Stage	甲 Yang Wood	丙 Yang Fire	戊 Yang Earth	庚 Yang Metal	壬 Yang Water
Birth	亥 Pig	**寅 Tiger**	**寅 Tiger**	巳 Snake	**申 Monkey**
Bath	子 Rat	卯 Rabbit	卯 Rabbit	午 Horse	酉 Rooster
Attire	丑 Ox	辰 Dragon	辰 Dragon	未 Sheep	戌 Dog
Arrival	寅 Tiger	巳 Snake	巳 Snake	申 Monkey	亥 Pig
Peak	卯 Rabbit	午 Horse	午 Horse	酉 Rooster	子 Rat
Ageing	辰 Dragon	未 Sheep	未 Sheep	戌 Dog	丑 Ox
Sickness	巳 Snake	申 Monkey	申 Monkey	亥 Pig	寅 Tiger
Death	午 Horse	酉 Rooster	酉 Rooster	子 Rat	卯 Rabbit
Tomb	未 Sheep	戌 Dog	戌 Dog	丑 Ox	辰 Dragon
End	申 Monkey	亥 Pig	亥 Pig	寅 Tiger	巳 Snake
Conception	酉 Rooster	子 Rat	子 Rat	卯 Rabbit	午 Horse
Nurture	戌 Dog	丑 Ox	丑 Ox	辰 Dragon	未 Sheep

Table 7.3 lists the 12 Life Stages for the Yin Resource Stems. The Life Stage to take into account is the Birth, which has been highlighted. Note that Yin Wood and Yin Metal do not sit on the Birth Branch as they are of the opposite polarity.

Table 7.3 12 Life Stages for the Yin Resource Stems

Stem Life Stage	乙 Yin Wood	丁 Yin Fire	己 Yin Earth	辛 Yin Metal	癸 Yin Water
Birth	午 Horse	**酉 Rooster**	**酉 Rooster**	子 Rat	**卯 Rabbit**
Bath	巳 Snake	申 Monkey	申 Monkey	亥 Pig	寅 Tiger
Attire	辰 Dragon	未 Sheep	未 Sheep	戌 Dog	丑 Ox
Arrival	卯 Rabbit	午 Horse	午 Horse	酉 Rooster	子 Rat
Peak	寅 Tiger	巳 Snake	巳 Snake	申 Monkey	亥 Pig
Ageing	丑 Ox	辰 Dragon	辰 Dragon	未 Sheep	戌 Dog
Sickness	子 Rat	卯 Rabbit	卯 Rabbit	午 Horse	酉 Rooster
Death	亥 Pig	寅 Tiger	寅 Tiger	巳 Snake	申 Monkey
Tomb	戌 Dog	丑 Ox	丑 Ox	辰 Dragon	未 Sheep
End	酉 Rooster	子 Rat	子 Rat	卯 Rabbit	午 Horse
Conception	申 Monkey	亥 Pig	亥 Pig	寅 Tiger	巳 Snake
Nurture	未 Sheep	戌 Dog	戌 Dog	丑 Ox	辰 Dragon

When the Resource element is sitting on the Birth Branch, the person's mother will be very capable, dutiful and caring. Table 7.4 indicates the Resource Sitting on the Birth Pillar.

Table 7.4 Resource Sitting on the Birth Pillar

Day Stem	Direct Resource	Indirect Resource
甲 Yang Wood	癸 Yin Water 卯 Rabbit	**壬 Yang Water** **申 Monkey**
乙 Yin Wood	壬 Yang Water 申 Monkey	癸 Yin Water 卯 Rabbit
丙 Yang Fire		
丁 Yin Fire		
戊 Yang Earth	丁 Yin Fire 酉 Rooster	丙 Yang Fire 寅 Tiger
己 Yin Earth	**丙 Yang Fire** **寅 Tiger**	丁 Yin Fire 酉 Rooster
庚 Yang Metal	己 Yin Earth 酉 Rooster	**戊 Yang Earth** **寅 Tiger**
辛 Yin Metal	戊 Yang Earth 寅 Tiger	己 Yin Earth 酉 Rooster
壬 Yang Water		
癸 Yin Water		

Only the pillars that are in bold can occur in the Hour Pillar.

The following examples illustrate each Resource Sitting on the Birth Pillar.

Example 7.1

Mila Kunis, American Actress,
August 14, 1983, 17:00 hours DST

Hour	Day	Month	Year
壬	甲	庚	癸
Yang Water	**Yang Wood**	Yang Metal	Yin Water
申	戌	申	亥
Monkey	Dog	Monkey	Pig

Kunis is a Yang Wood Day Stem. The Resource Sitting on the Birth Pillar Yang Water Monkey is present in the Hour. Her mother is Elvira, a physics teacher who runs a pharmacy. The family moved from the Soviet Union to the United States in 1991 (Yin Metal Sheep year). Kunis's parents gave up their jobs to give her and her brother a better future.

Example 7.2

Harvey Weinstein, American Film Producer,
March 19, 1952, 21:45 hours

Hour	Day	Month	Year
乙	甲	癸	壬
Yin Wood	**Yang Wood**	**Yin Water**	Yang Water
亥	子	卯	辰
Pig	Rat	**Rabbit**	Dragon

Weinstein is a Yang Wood Day Stem. The Resource Sitting on the Birth Pillar Yin Water Rabbit is present in the Month. His mother Miriam migrated with her parents from Poland to New York City. Weinstein's family grew up in a housing co-op in New York City.

Example 7.3

Anthony Perkins, American Actor and Director,
April 4, 1932, 09:00 hours

Hour	Day	Month	Year
辛	乙	癸	壬
Yin Metal	**Yin Wood**	**Yin Water**	**Yang Water**
巳	未	卯	申
Snake	Sheep	**Rabbit**	**Monkey**

Perkins is a Yin Wood Day Stem. There are two Resource Sitting on the Birth Pillars in his chart, Yang Water Monkey in the Year and Yin Water Rabbit in the Month. His mother Janet was very close to him as his father, actor Osgood, was absent.

Example 7.4

Jessica Biel, American Actress and Model,
March 3, 1982, 00:56 hours

Hour	Day	Month	Year
丙	乙	癸	壬
Yang Fire	**Yin Wood**	**Yin Water**	Yang Water
子	酉	卯	戌
Rat	Rooster	**Rabbit**	Dog

Biel is a Yin Wood Day Stem. The Resource Sitting on the Birth Pillar Yin Water Rabbit is present in the Month. Her mother Kimberly is a homemaker and spiritual healer. Biel's family moved frequently during her childhood, living in Texas, Connecticut and Illinois before settling in Boulder, Colorado.

Example 7.5

Chaz Bono, American Writer, March 4, 1969, 00:55 hours

Hour	Day	Month	Year
壬	戊	丙	己
Yang Water	**Yang Earth**	**Yang Fire**	Yin Earth
子	寅	寅	酉
Rat	Tiger	**Tiger**	Rooster

Bono is a Yang Earth Day Stem. The Resource Sitting on the Birth Pillar Yang Fire Tiger is present in the Month. His mother, Cher is a singer and actress, who is very supportive of his coming out and gender transition.

Example 7.6

Seann William Scott, American Actor, October 3, 1976, 03:50 hours DST

Hour	Day	Month	Year
癸	戊	丁	丙
Yin Water	**Yang Earth**	**Yin Fire**	Yang Fire
丑	子	酉	辰
Ox	Rat	**Rooster**	Dragon

Scott is a Yang Earth Day Stem. The Resource Sitting on the Birth Pillar Yin Fire Rooster is present in the Month. He is the youngest of seven children of Patricia Anne Simons and William Frank Scott.

Example 7.7

Marion Cotillard, French Actress, September 30, 1975, 04:50 hours

Hour	Day	Month	Year
丙	己	乙	乙
Yang Fire	**Yin Earth**	Yin Wood	Yin Wood
寅	卯	酉	卯
Tiger	Rabbit	Rooster	Rabbit

Cotillard is a Yin Earth Day Stem. The Resource Sitting on the Birth Pillar Yang Fire Tiger is present in the Hour. Her mother Monique Niseema Theillaud is an actress and drama teacher. Cotillard began acting during her childhood.

Example 7.8

Alexander Skarsgard, Swedish Actor, August 25, 1976, 04:47 hours

Hour	Day	Month	Year
丙	己	丁	丙
Yang Fire	**Yin Earth**	**Yin Fire**	Yang Fire
寅	酉	酉	辰
Tiger	Rooster	**Rooster**	Dragon

Skarsgard is a Yin Earth Day Stem. There are two Resource Sitting on the Birth Pillars in his chart, Yin Fire Rooster in the Month and Yang Fire Tiger in the Hour. He is the eldest of six children of his mother, physician An and his father, actor Stellan Skarsgard.

Example 7.9

Arnold Schwarzenegger, Austrian-American Actor and Politician, July 30, 1947, 04:10 hours

Hour	Day	Month	Year
戊	庚	丁	丁
Yang Earth	**Yang Metal**	Yin Fire	Yin Fire
寅	戌	未	亥
Tiger	Dog	Sheep	Pig

Schwarzenegger is a Yang Metal Day Stem. The Resource Sitting on the Birth Pillar Yang Earth Tiger is present in the Hour. He is the second son of Aurelia and Gustav. Schwarzenegger had a good relationship with his mother and a distant one with his father.

Example 7.10

Hilary Duff, American Actress and Singer, September 28, 1987, 15:56 hours DST

Hour	Day	Month	Year
癸	庚	己	丁
Yin Water	**Yang Metal**	**Yin Earth**	Yin Fire
未	辰	酉	卯
Sheep	Dragon	**Rooster**	Rabbit

Duff is a Yang Metal Day Stem. The Resource Sitting on the Birth Pillar Yin Earth Rooster is present in the Month. Her mother Susan is a homemaker turned film and music producer. Duff and her older sister Haylie were encouraged by their mother to act and model while being home schooled.

Example 7.11

Bernie Madoff, American Financier,
April 29, 1938, 13:50 hours DST

Hour	Day	Month	Year
甲	辛	丙	戊
Yang Wood	**Yin Metal**	Yang Fire	**Yang Earth**
午	卯	辰	寅
Horse	Rabbit	Dragon	**Tiger**

Madoff is a Yin Metal Day Stem. The Resource Sitting on the Birth Pillar Yang Earth Tiger is present in the Year. He was the second of three children of Sylvia and Ralph, a plumber and stockbroker.

Example 7.12

Gwen Stefani, American Singer-Songwriter and Actress,
October 3, 1969, 14:09 hours

Hour	Day	Month	Year
乙	辛	癸	己
Yin Wood	**Yin Metal**	Yin Water	**Yin Earth**
未	亥	酉	酉
Sheep	Pig	Rooster	**Rooster**

Stefani is a Yin Metal Day Stem. The Resource Sitting on the Birth Pillar Yin Earth Rooster is present in the Year. She is the second of four children. Her mother Patti was an accountant before becoming a housewife.

Resource Sitting on the Seven Killings

When the Resource element (both Direct and Indirect) is Sitting on a Branch which has the Seven Killings hidden within it, the person will be assertive and courageous.

Table 7.5 lists the Seven Killings for the Day Stems and the Branch of the same polarity where the Seven Killings is hidden.

Table 7.5 Day Stem and Seven Killings

Day Stem	Seven Killings
甲 Yang Wood	庚 Yang Metal
乙 Yin Wood	辛 Yin Metal
丙 Yang Fire	壬 Yang Water
丁 Yin Fire	癸 Yin Water
戊 Yang Earth	甲 Yang Wood
己 Yin Earth	乙 Yin Wood
庚 Yang Metal	丙 Yang Fire
辛 Yin Metal	丁 Yin Fire
壬 Yang Water	戊 Yang Earth
癸 Yin Water	己 Yin Earth

Table 7.6 lists the Day Stem with the Resource Sitting on the Seven Killings Pillars. Both Direct and Indirect Resource are considered.

Table 7.6 Day Stem with Resource Sitting on Seven Killings Pillars

Day Stem	Direct Resource	Indirect Resource
甲 Yang Wood	癸 Yin Water 巳 Snake	**壬 Yang Water** **申 Monkey**
乙 Yin Wood	壬 Yang Water 戌 Dog	癸 Yin Water 丑 Ox 癸 Yin Water 酉 Rooster

丙 Yang Fire	乙 Yin Wood 亥 Pig	甲 Yang Wood 申 Monkey
丁 Yin Fire	甲 Yang Wood 子 Rat **甲 Yang Wood** **辰 Dragon**	乙 Yin Wood 丑 Ox
戊 Yang Earth	丁 Yin Fire 亥 Pig	丙 Yang Fire 寅 Tiger
己 Yin Earth	丙 Yang Fire 辰 Dragon	**丁 Yin Fire** 丁 Yin Fire **卯 Rabbit** 未 Sheep
庚 Yang Metal	己 Yin Earth 巳 Snake	**戊 Yang Earth** **寅 Tiger**
辛 Yin Metal	戊 Yang Earth 午 Horse **戊 Yang Earth** **戌 Dog**	己 Yin Earth 未 Sheep
壬 Yang Water	辛 Yin Metal 巳 Snake	庚 Yang Metal 寅 Tiger 庚 Yang Metal 辰 Dragon 庚 Yang Metal 申 Monkey **庚 Yang Metal** **戌 Dog**
癸 Yin Water	辛 Yin Metal 辛 Yin Metal 丑 Ox 未 Sheep	庚 Yang Metal 午 Horse

Only the Pillars that are in bold can occur in the Hour Pillar.

The following examples illustrate each Resource Sitting on the Seven Killings Pillar.

Example 7.13

Cher, American Singer and Actress, May 20, 1946, 07:25 hours

Hour	Day	Month	Year
戊	**甲**	**癸**	丙
Yang Earth	**Yang Wood**	**Yin Water**	Yang Fire
辰	午	**巳**	戌
Dragon	Horse	**Snake**	Dog
		庚 **Yang Metal**	

Cher is a Yang Wood Day Stem. The Resource Sitting on the Seven Killings Pillar Yin Water Snake is present in the Month. The Seven Killings Yang Metal is hidden in the Snake. At age 16, Cher dropped out of school, moved to Los Angeles and took acting classes and worked to support herself. She then met performer Sonny Bono, who introduced her to producer Phil Spector.

Example 7.14

Adam Levine, American Singer-Songwriter *Maroon 5*, March 18, 1979, 15:24 hours

Hour	Day	Month	Year
壬	**甲**	丁	己
Yang Water	**Yang Wood**	Yin Fire	Yin Earth
申	申	卯	未
Monkey	Monkey	Rabbit	Sheep
庚 **Yang Metal**			

Levine is a Yang Wood Day Stem. The Resource Sitting on the Seven Killings Pillar Yang Water Monkey is present in the Hour. The Seven Killings Yang Metal is hidden in the Monkey. Yang Water Monkey is also the Resource Sitting on the Birth Pillar. Levine's mother Patsy, an admissions counselor started him on his musical career. He worked as a writer's assistant on the television show *Judging Amy* before his band *Maroon 5* found success.

Example 7.15

Emma Stone, American Actress,
November 6, 1988, 00:50 hours

Hour	Day	Month	Year
丙	乙	壬	戊
Yang Fire	**Yin Wood**	**Yang Water**	Yang Earth
子	丑	戌	午
Rat	Ox	**Dog**	Horse
		辛 **Yin Metal**	

Stone is a Yin Wood Day Stem. The Resource Sitting on the Seven Killings Pillar Yang Water Dog is present in the Month. The Seven Killings Yin Metal is hidden in the Dog. She dropped out from high school and moved to California with her mother to pursue acting. Stone worked part time at a dog treat bakery before landing her first film roles.

Example 7.16

David Chokachi, American Actor,
January 16, 1968, 13:03 hours

Hour	Day	Month	Year
癸	乙	癸	戊
Yin Water	**Yin Wood**	**Yin Water**	Yang Earth
未	酉	丑	申
Sheep	Rooster	**Ox**	Monkey
		辛 **Yin Metal**	

Chokachi is a Yin Wood Day Stem. The Resource Sitting on the Seven Killings Pillar Yin Water Ox is present in the Month. The Seven Killings Yin Metal is hidden in the Ox. Chockachi graduated from Bates College in Maine with a degree in political science before he pursued an acting career.

Example 7.17

Leonard Cohen, Canadian Singer and Poet,
September 21, 1934, 06:45 hours DST

Hour	Day	Month	Year
戊	乙	癸	甲
Yang Earth	**Yin Wood**	**Yin Water**	Yang Wood
寅	未	酉	戌
Tiger	Sheep	**Rooster**	Dog
		辛 **Yin Metal**	

Cohen is a Yin Wood Day Stem. The Resource Sitting on the Seven Killings Pillar Yin Water Rooster is present in the Month. The Seven Killings Yin Metal is hidden in the Rooster. He started writing poetry while working on various odd jobs before writing and recording songs.

Example 7.18

Adam Brody, American Actor,
December 15, 1979, 09:52 hours

Hour	Day	Month	Year
癸	丙	乙	己
Yin Water	**Yang Fire**	**Yin Wood**	Yin Earth
巳	辰	亥	未
Snake	Dragon	**Pig**	Sheep
		壬 **Yang Water**	

Brody is a Yang Fire Day Stem. The Resource Sitting on the Seven Killings Pillar Yin Wood Pig is present in the Month. The Seven Killings Yang Water is hidden in the Pig. He dropped out of college at the age of nineteen and moved to Hollywood to become an actor. After a year of training and auditioning, Brody had his first role in the television film *Growing Up Brady*.

Example 7.19

J.K. Rowling, British Author,
July 31, 1965, 21:10 hours DST

Hour	Day	Month	Year
戊	丙	甲	乙
Yang Earth	**Yang Fire**	**Yang Wood**	Yin Wood
戌	戌	申	巳
Dog	Dog	**Monkey**	Snake
		壬 **Yang Water**	

Rowling is a Yang Fire Day Stem. The Resource Sitting on the Seven Killings Pillar Yang Wood Monkey is present in the Month. The Seven Killings Yang Water is hidden in the Monkey. Before achieving success with the Harry Potter novels, Rowling was living on state assistance as a single mother, having earned a teaching certificate and a degree in French.

Example 7.20

Infanta Elena of Spain, Spanish Royalty,
December 20, 1963, 14:10 hours

Hour	Day	Month	Year
丁	丁	甲	癸
Yin Fire	**Yin Fire**	**Yang Wood**	Yin Water
未	酉	子	卯
Sheep	Rooster	**Rat**	Rabbit
		癸 **Yin Water**	

Elena is a Yin Fire Day Stem. The Resource Sitting on the Seven Killings Pillar Yang Wood Rat is present in the Month. The Seven Killings Yin Water is hidden in the Rat. Elena is third in line of succession to the Spanish throne. She studied French literature.

Example 7.21

Diane Warren, American Songwriter, September 7, 1956, 08:24 hours

Hour	Day	Month	Year
甲	丁	丁	丙
Yang Wood	**Yin Fire**	Yin Fire	Yang Fire
辰	丑	酉	申
Dragon	Ox	Rooster	Monkey
癸 **Yin Water**			

Warren is a Yin Fire Day Stem. The Resource Sitting on the Seven Killings Pillar Yang Wood Dragon is present in the Hour. The Seven Killings Yin Water is hidden in the Dragon. She graduated from California State University, Northridge and focused on her songwriting skills. Her first hit, Laura Branigan's *Solitaire* was in 1983 (Yin Water Pig year), five years after she graduated.

Example 7.22

Will Young, British Singer and Actor, January 20, 1979, 21:55 hours

Hour	Day	Month	Year
辛	丁	乙	戊
Yin Metal	**Yin Fire**	**Yin Wood**	Yang Earth
亥	亥	丑	午
Pig	Pig	**Ox**	Horse
		癸 **Yin Water**	

Young is a Yin Fire Day Stem. The Resource Sitting on the Seven Killings Pillar Yin Wood Ox is present in the Month. The Seven Killings Yin Water is hidden in the Ox. Young graduated from the University of Exeter with a degree in politics. He then enrolled in the Arts Educational School in Chiswick, London before he won the first season of the television reality singing show *Pop Idol*.

Example 7.23

Anni-Frid Lyngstad, Norwegian-Swedish Singer *ABBA*, November 15, 1945, 04:00 hours

Hour	Day	Month	Year
甲	戊	丁	乙
Yang Wood	**Yang Earth**	**Yin Fire**	Yin Wood
寅	子	亥	酉
Tiger	Rat	**Pig**	Rooster
		甲 **Yang Wood**	

Lyngstad is a Yang Earth Day Stem. The Resource Sitting on the Seven Killings Pillar Yin Fire Pig is present in the Month. The Seven Killings Yang Wood is hidden in the Pig. She was brought up by her maternal grandmother as her parents died early. At the age of 13, Lyngstad gained her first job as a dance band singer. She then won the Swedish national talent competition *New Faces* at the age of 22.

Example 7.24

Hugh Hefner, American Magazine Publisher,
April 9, 1926, 16:20 hours

Hour	Day	Month	Year
庚	戊	辛	丙
Yang Metal	**Yang Earth**	Yin Metal	**Yang Fire**
申	辰	卯	寅
Monkey	Dragon	Rabbit	**Tiger**
			甲 **Yang Wood**

Hefner is a Yang Earth Day Stem. The Resource Sitting on the Seven Killings Pillar Yang Fire Tiger is present in the Year. The Seven Killings Yang Wood is hidden in the Tiger. The Yang Fire Tiger is also The Resource Sitting on the Birth Pillar. Hefner's mother Grace was a teacher. He graduated from the University of Illinois in Urbana-Champaign with a Bachelor of Arts in Psychology. Hefner left his job as a copywriter and gathered money from investors to launch *Playboy* in December 1953 (Yin Water Snake year).

Example 7.25

Celine Dion, Canadian Singer, March 30, 1968, 12:15 hours

Hour	Day	Month	Year
庚	己	丙	戊
Yang Metal	**Yin Earth**	**Yang Fire**	Yang Earth
午	亥	辰	申
Horse	Pig	**Dragon**	Monkey
		乙 **Yin Wood**	

Dion is a Yin Earth Day Stem. The Resource Sitting on the Seven Killings Pillar Yang Fire Dragon is present in the Month. The Seven Killings Yin Wood is hidden in the Dragon. She is the youngest of 14 children and performed with her siblings as a child. At the age of 14, she won the award for Top Performer at the Yamaha World Popular Song Festival in Tokyo, Japan.

Example 7.26

Jean-Claude Van Damme, Belgian Actor and Martial Artist, October 18, 1960, 06:45 hours

Hour	Day	Month	Year
丁	己	乙	庚
Yin Fire	**Yin Earth**	Yin Wood	Yang Metal
卯	卯	酉	子
Rabbit	Rabbit	Rooster	Rat
乙 **Yin Wood**			

Van Damme is a Yin Earth Day Stem. The Resource Sitting on the Seven Killings Pillar Yin Fire Rabbit is present in the Hour. The Seven Killings Yin Wood is hidden in the Rabbit. Van Damme was a karate professional who had also studied ballet, Taekwondo and Muay Thai before he started his acting career.

Example 7.27

Geri Halliwell, English Singer *Spice Girls*, August 6, 1972, 14:30 hours

Hour	Day	Month	Year
辛	己	丁	壬
Yin Metal	**Yin Earth**	**Yin Fire**	Yang Water
未	巳	未	子
Sheep	Snake	**Sheep**	Rat
		乙 **Yin Wood**	

Halliwell is a Yin Earth Day Stem. The Resource Sitting on the Seven Killings Pillar Yin Fire Sheep is present in the Month. The Seven Killings Yin Wood is hidden in the Sheep. Before starting her singing career, she worked as a nightclub dancer in Majorca, a presenter on Turkish television and a glamour model.

Example 7.28

Anne Heche, American Actress, May 25, 1969, 16:51 hours

Hour	Day	Month	Year
甲	庚	己	己
Yang Wood	**Yang Metal**	Yin Earth	Yin Earth
申	子	巳	酉
Monkey	Rat	**Snake**	Rooster
		丙 **Yang Fire**	

Heche is a Yang Metal Day Stem. The Resource Sitting on the Seven Killings Pillar Yin Earth Snake is present in the Month. The Seven Killings Yang Fire is hidden in the Snake. Heche left high school shortly before graduation when she was offered a role on the daytime soap opera *Another World*.

Example 7.29

Jennifer Lopez, American Actress and Singer,
July 24, 1969, 05:49 hours DST

Hour	Day	Month	Year
戊	庚	辛	己
Yang Earth	**Yang Metal**	Yin Metal	Yin Earth
寅	子	未	酉
Tiger	Rat	Sheep	Rooster
丙 **Yang Fire**			

Lopez is a Yang Metal Day Stem. The Resource Sitting on the Seven Killings Pillar Yang Earth Tiger is present in the Hour. The Seven Killings Yang Fire is hidden in the Tiger. Yang Earth Tiger is also the Resource Sitting on the Birth Pillar. Lopez dropped out of college to pursue a dancing career. She worked as a professional dancer for a few years while attending acting classes.

Example 7.30

James Franco, American Actor, April 19, 1978, 19:04 hours

Hour	Day	Month	Year
戊	辛	丙	戊
Yang Earth	**Yin Metal**	Yang Fire	**Yang Earth**
戌	亥	辰	午
Dog	Pig	Dragon	Horse
丁 **Yin Fire**			丁 **Yin Fire**

Franco is a Yin Metal Day Stem. There are two Resource Sitting on the Seven Killings Pillars present in his chart, Yang Earth Horse in the Year and Yang Earth Dog in the Hour. The Seven Killings Yin Fire is hidden in the Horse and Dog. Franco dropped out of the University of California, Los Angeles to pursue an acting career. He worked part-time at McDonalds to support himself while taking acting classes.

Example 7.31

Sylvester Stallone, American Actor,
July 6, 1946, 19:20 hours

Hour	Day	Month	Year
戊	辛	乙	丙
Yang Earth	**Yin Metal**	Yin Wood	Yang Fire
戌	巳	未	戌
Dog	Snake	Sheep	Dog
丁 **Yin Fire**			

Stallone is a Yin Metal Day Stem. The Resource Sitting on the Seven Killings Pillar Yang Earth Dog is present in the Hour. The Seven Killings Yin Fire is hidden in the Dog. Stallone worked in odd jobs as a zoo cleaner and a movie theatre usher before his acting career took off.

Example 7.32

Lance Bass, American Singer and Actor *NSYNC*,
May 4, 1979, 13:20 hours DST

Hour	Day	Month	Year
甲	辛	己	己
Yang Wood	**Yin Metal**	Yin Earth	**Yin Earth**
午	未	巳	未
Horse	Sheep	Snake	**Sheep**
			丁 **Yin Fire**

Bass is a Yin Metal Day Stem. The Resource Sitting on the Seven Killings Pillar Yin Earth Sheep is present in the Year. The Seven Killings Yin Fire is hidden in the Sheep. Bass left high school to join the band *NSYNC* full time. He moved to Munich, Germany to tour Europe and record their first album.

Example 7.33

Dave Franco, American Actor,
June 12, 1985, 21:18 hours DST

Hour	Day	Month	Year
庚	壬	辛	乙
Yang Metal	**Yang Water**	**Yin Metal**	Yin Wood
戌	午	巳	丑
Dog	Horse	**Snake**	Ox
戊 Yang Earth		戊 Yang Earth	

Franco is a Yang Water Day Stem. There are two Resource Sitting on the Seven Killings Pillars in his chart, Yin Metal Snake in the Month and Yang Metal Dog in the Hour. The Seven Killings Yang Earth is hidden in the Snake and the Dog. Franco studied at University of Southern California and was planning a career as a high school teacher before being guided by his brother James's manager to an acting career.

Example 7.34

Anne, Princess Royal,
British Royalty, August 15, 1950, 11:50 hours DST

Hour	Day	Month	Year
乙	壬	甲	庚
Yin Wood	**Yang Water**	Yang Wood	**Yang Metal**
巳	午	申	寅
Snake	Horse	Monkey	**Tiger**
			戊 Yang Earth

Anne is a Yang Water Day Stem. The Resource Sitting on the Seven Killings Pillar Yang Metal Tiger is present in the Year. The Seven Killings Yang Earth is hidden in the Tiger. Anne is a respected equestrian and the first member of the British Royal Family to have competed in the Olympic Games.

Example 7.35

Chuck Norris, American Actor and Martial Artist,
March 10, 1940, 03:30 hours

Hour	Day	Month	Year
壬	壬	己	庚
Yang Water	**Yang Water**	Yin Earth	**Yang Metal**
寅	子	卯	辰
Tiger	Rat	Rabbit	**Dragon**
			戊 **Yang Earth**

Norris is a Yang Water Day Stem. The Resource Sitting on the Seven Killings Pillar Yang Metal Dragon is present in the Year. The Seven Killings Yang Earth is hidden in the Dragon. Norris served four years of military service as an Air Policeman and was also a martial arts champion before launching his acting career.

Example 7.36

Liam Payne, English Singer-Songwriter *One Direction*,
August 29, 1993, 13:00 hours DST

Hour	Day	Month	Year
丙	壬	庚	癸
Yang Fire	**Yang Water**	**Yang Metal**	Yin Water
午	午	申	酉
Horse	Horse	**Monkey**	Rooster
		戊 **Yang Earth**	

Payne is a Yang Water Day Stem. The Resource Sitting on the Seven Killings Pillar Yang Metal Monkey is present in the Month. The Seven Killings Yang Earth is hidden in the Monkey. At the age of 14, Payne auditioned for *The X Factor* unsuccessfully and was told to come back in two years. In 2010 (Yang Metal Tiger year), he was placed with four other singers to form the band *One Direction*, which ended up third on *The X Factor*.

Example 7.37

Robert Redford, American Actor and Director, August 18, 1936, 20:02 hours

Hour	Day	Month	Year
庚	壬	丙	丙
Yang Metal	**Yang Water**	Yang Fire	Yang Fire
戌	申	申	子
Dog	Monkey	Monkey	Rat
戊 **Yang Earth**			

Redford is a Yang Water Day Stem. The Resource Sitting on the Seven Killings Pillar Yang Metal Dog is present in the Hour. The Seven Killings Yang Earth is hidden in the Dog. Redford lost his college half-scholarship due to his drinking. He then travelled around Europe and attended classes at the American Academy of Dramatic Arts. He then started his acting career on Broadway and television.

Example 7.38

Meryl Streep, American Actress, June 22, 1949, 08:05 hours

Hour	Day	Month	Year
丙	癸	庚	己
Yang Fire	**Yin Water**	**Yang Metal**	Yin Earth
辰	未	午	丑
Dragon	Sheep	**Horse**	Ox
		己 **Yin Earth**	

Streep is a Yin Water Day Stem. The Resource Sitting on the Seven Killings Pillar Yang Metal Horse is present in the Month. The Seven Killings Yin Earth is hidden in the Horse. She received her Bachelor of Arts from Vassar College before receiving a Masters of Fine Arts from Yale. Streep then moved to New York City starting her acting career on Broadway.

Example 7.39

Michael J. Fox, American Actor and Comedian, June 9, 1961, 00:15 hours

Hour	Day	Month	Year
壬	癸	癸	辛
Yang Water	**Yin Water**	Yin Water	**Yin Metal**
子	酉	巳	丑
Rat	Rooster	Snake	**Ox**
			己 **Yin Earth**

Fox is a Yin Water Day Stem. The Resource Sitting on the Seven Killings Pillar Yin Metal Ox is present in the Year. The Seven Killings Yin Earth is hidden in the Ox. At the age of 18, Fox moved from Vancouver to Los Angeles to further his acting career.

Example 7.40

Shane Filan, Irish Singer *Westlife*, July 5, 1979, 08:45 hours

Hour	Day	Month	Year
丙	癸	辛	己
Yang Fire	**Yin Water**	**Yin Metal**	Yin Earth
辰	酉	未	未
Dragon	Rooster	**Sheep**	Sheep
		己 **Yin Earth**	

Filan is a Yin Water Day Stem. The Resource Sitting on the Seven Killings Pillar Yin Metal Sheep is present in the Month. The Seven Killings Yin Earth is hidden in the Sheep. Filan started singing with future *Westlife* bandmates Mark Feehily and Kian Egan in a band *Six* as *One* before securing Louis Walsh as their manager.

Summary

In summary, what to look for in a chart with regard to the Resource:

1. Resource Sitting on the Birth Pillar.
2. Resource Sitting on the Seven Killings Pillar.

捌

Chapter Eight

Chapter Eight Rivals

Rivals refer to those who have the same element as the Self. They can be divided into Siblings, which is the same polarity as the Day Stem and Rob Wealth, which is the opposite polarity of the Day Stem.

Table 8.1 indicates the Day Stem and corresponding Siblings and Rob Wealth.

Table 8.1 Siblings and Rob Wealth

Day Stem	Sibling	Rob Wealth
甲 Yang Wood	甲 Yang Wood	乙 Yin Wood
乙 Yin Wood	乙 Yin Wood	甲 Yang Wood
丙 Yang Fire	丙 Yang Fire	丁 Yin Fire
丁 Yin Fire	丁 Yin Fire	丙 Yang Fire
戊 Yang Earth	戊 Yang Earth	己 Yin Earth
己 Yin Earth	己 Yin Earth	戊 Yang Earth
庚 Yang Metal	庚 Yang Metal	辛 Yin Metal
辛 Yin Metal	辛 Yin Metal	庚 Yang Metal
壬 Yang Water	壬 Yang Water	癸 Yin Water
癸 Yin Water	癸 Yin Water	壬 Yang Water

With regard to interpretation, there is no distinction between Sibling and Rob Wealth. They are referred to collectively as Rivals.

Rivals Sitting on the Birth, Arrival or Peak

When a Rival within the chart is Sitting on the Birth, Arrival or Peak (of the 12 Life Stages), then there is a large number of siblings. There are five Rival Yang Stems and five Rival Yin Stems to consider.

For Yang Rivals of the Day Stems, consider Table 8.2. For Yin Rivals of the Day Stems, look up Table 8.3.

Table 8.2 lists the 12 Life Stages for the Yang Rival Stems. The Life Stages to take into account are the Birth, Arrival or Peak, which have been highlighted.

Table 8.2 12 Life Stages for the Yang Rival Stems

Stem Life Stage	甲 Yang Wood	丙 Yang Fire	戊 Yang Earth	庚 Yang Metal	壬 Yang Water
Birth	亥 Pig	寅 **Tiger**	寅 **Tiger**	巳 Snake	申 **Monkey**
Bath	子 Rat	卯 Rabbit	卯 Rabbit	午 Horse	酉 Rooster
Attire	丑 Ox	辰 Dragon	辰 Dragon	未 Sheep	戌 Dog
Arrival	寅 **Tiger**	巳 Snake	巳 Snake	申 **Monkey**	亥 Pig
Peak	卯 Rabbit	午 **Horse**	午 **Horse**	酉 Rooster	子 **Rat**
Ageing	辰 Dragon	未 Sheep	未 Sheep	戌 Dog	丑 Ox
Sickness	巳 Snake	申 Monkey	申 Monkey	亥 Pig	寅 Tiger
Death	午 Horse	酉 Rooster	酉 Rooster	子 Rat	卯 Rabbit
Tomb	未 Sheep	戌 Dog	戌 Dog	丑 Ox	辰 Dragon
End	申 Monkey	亥 Pig	亥 Pig	寅 Tiger	巳 Snake
Conception	酉 Rooster	子 Rat	子 Rat	卯 Rabbit	午 Horse
Nurture	戌 Dog	丑 Ox	丑 Ox	辰 Dragon	未 Sheep

Table 8.3 lists the 12 Life Stages for the Yin Rival Stems. The Life Stages to take into account are the Birth, Arrival or Peak, which have been highlighted.

Table 8.3 12 Life Stages for the Yin Rival Stems

Stem Life Stage	乙 Yin Wood	丁 Yin Fire	己 Yin Earth	辛 Yin Metal	癸 Yin Water
Birth	午 Horse	酉 **Rooster**	酉 **Rooster**	子 Rat	卯 **Rabbit**
Bath	巳 Snake	申 Monkey	申 Monkey	亥 Pig	寅 Tiger
Attire	辰 Dragon	未 Sheep	未 Sheep	戌 Dog	丑 Ox
Arrival	卯 **Rabbit**	午 Horse	午 Horse	酉 **Rooster**	子 Rat
Peak	寅 Tiger	巳 **Snake**	巳 **Snake**	申 Monkey	亥 **Pig**
Ageing	丑 Ox	辰 Dragon	辰 Dragon	未 Sheep	戌 Dog
Sickness	子 Rat	卯 Rabbit	卯 Rabbit	午 Horse	酉 Rooster
Death	亥 Pig	寅 Tiger	寅 Tiger	巳 Snake	申 Monkey
Tomb	戌 Dog	丑 Ox	丑 Ox	辰 Dragon	未 Sheep
End	酉 Rooster	子 Rat	子 Rat	卯 Rabbit	午 Horse
Conception	申 Monkey	亥 Pig	亥 Pig	寅 Tiger	巳 Snake
Nurture	未 Sheep	戌 Dog	戌 Dog	丑 Ox	辰 Dragon

Table 8.4 lists the Day Stems and Rivals on Birth, Peak or Arrival.

Table 8.4 Day Stems and Rivals on the Birth, Peak or Arrival

Day Stem	Rivals on Birth, Peak or Arrival	Rivals on Birth, Peak or Arrival
甲 Yang Wood	甲 Yang Wood 寅 Tiger	乙 Yin Wood 卯 Rabbit
乙 Yin Wood	乙 Yin Wood 卯 Rabbit	甲 Yang Wood 寅 Tiger
丙 Yang Fire	丙 Yang Fire 丙 Yang Fire 寅 Tiger 午 Horse	丁 Yin Fire 丁 **Yin Fire** 巳 Snake 酉 **Rooster**
丁 Yin Fire	丁 Yin Fire 丁 Yin Fire 巳 Snake 酉 Rooster	丙 Yang Fire 丙 **Yang Fire** 寅 Tiger 午 **Horse**
戊 Yang Earth	戊 Yang Earth 戊 **Yang Earth** 寅 Tiger 午 **Horse**	己 Yin Earth 己 Yin Earth 巳 Snake 酉 Rooster
己 Yin Earth	己 **Yin Earth** 己 Yin Earth 巳 **Snake** 酉 Rooster	戊 Yang Earth 戊 Yang Earth 寅 Tiger 午 Horse
庚 Yang Metal	庚 Yang Metal 申 Monkey	辛 Yin Metal 酉 Rooster
辛 Yin Metal	辛 Yin Metal 酉 Rooster	庚 Yang Metal 申 Monkey
壬 Yang Water	壬 Yang Water 壬 Yang Water 申 Monkey 子 Rat	癸 Yin Water 癸 Yin Water 卯 Rabbit 亥 Pig
癸 Yin Water	癸 Yin Water 癸 **Yin Water** 卯 Rabbit 亥 **Pig**	壬 Yang Water 壬 **Yang Water** 申 Monkey 子 **Rat**

The Pillars that are highlighted can occur in the Hour Pillar.

The following examples illustrate all the Rivals Sitting on the Birth, Peak or Arrival Pillars.

Example 8.1

George Harrison, English Singer-Songwriter and Musician
Beatles, February 25, 1943, 00:10 hours

Hour	Day	Month	Year
甲	甲	甲	癸
Yang Wood	**Yang Wood**	**Yang Wood**	Yin Water
子	寅	寅	未
Rat	Tiger	**Tiger**	Sheep

Harrison is a Yang Wood Day Stem. The Yang Rival Sitting on the Arrival Pillar Yang Wood Tiger is present in the Month. Harrison was the youngest of four children, with two brothers and a sister.

Example 8.2

Kate Winslet, English Actress, October 5, 1975, 07:15 hours DST

Hour	Day	Month	Year
丁	甲	丙	乙
Yin Fire	**Yang Wood**	Yang Fire	**Yin Wood**
卯	申	戌	卯
Rabbit	Monkey	Dog	**Rabbit**

Winslet is a Yang Wood Day Stem. The Yin Rival Sitting on the Peak Pillar Yin Wood Rabbit is present in the Year. Winslet has two sisters and a younger brother.

Example 8.3

Mel Brown, English Singer and Television Personality *Spice Girls*, May 29, 1975, 17:59 hours DST

Hour	Day	Month	Year
甲	乙	辛	乙
Yang Wood	**Yin Wood**	Yin Metal	**Yin Wood**
申	亥	巳	卯
Monkey	Pig	Snake	**Rabbit**

Brown is a Yin Wood Day Stem. The Yin Rival Sitting on the Peak Pillar Yin Wood Rabbit is present in the Year. Brown has a younger sister, Danielle.

Example 8.4

Robbie Williams, English Singer-Songwriter *Take That*, February 13, 1974, 17:40 hours

Hour	Day	Month	Year
乙	乙	甲	甲
Yin Wood	**Yin Wood**	**Yang Wood**	**Yang Wood**
酉	酉	寅	寅
Rooster	Rooster	**Tiger**	**Tiger**

Williams is a Yin Wood Day Stem. The Yang Rival Sitting on the Arrival Pillar Yang Wood Tiger is present in the Year and Month. Williams has an older sister, Sally.

Example 8.5

Ron Howard, American Director and Actor, March 1, 1954, 09:03 hours

Hour	Day	Month	Year
癸	丙	丙	甲
Yin Water	**Yang Fire**	**Yang Fire**	Yang Wood
巳	辰	寅	午
Snake	Dragon	**Tiger**	Horse

Howard is a Yang Fire Day Stem. The Yang Rival Sitting on the Birth Pillar Yang Fire Tiger is present in the Month. Howard has a younger brother, Clint.

Example 8.6

Frida Kahlo, Mexican Painter, July 6, 1907, 08:30 hours

Hour	Day	Month	Year
壬	丙	丙	丁
Yang Water	**Yang Fire**	**Yang Fire**	Yin Fire
辰	辰	午	未
Dragon	Dragon	**Horse**	Sheep

Kahlo is a Yang Fire Day Stem. The Yang Rival Sitting on the Peak Pillar Yang Fire Horse is present in the Month. Kahlo had two older sisters and a younger sister.

Example 8.7

Milo Ventimiglia, American Actor,
July 8, 1977, 23:41 hours DST

Hour	Day	Month	Year
己	丙	丙	丁
Yin Earth	**Yang Fire**	**Yang Fire**	**Yin Fire**
亥	寅	午	巳
Pig	Tiger	**Horse**	**Snake**

Ventimiglia is a Yang Fire Day Stem. The Yang Rival Sitting on the Peak Pillar Yang Fire Horse is present in the Month. The Yin Rival Sitting on the Peak Yin Fire Snake is present in the Year. Ventimiglia has two older sisters, Leslie and Laurel.

Example 8.8

Steven Spielberg, American Film Director,
December 18, 1946, 18:16 hours

Hour	Day	Month	Year
丁	丙	庚	丙
Yin Fire	**Yang Fire**	Yang Metal	Yang Fire
酉	寅	子	戌
Rooster	Tiger	Rat	Dog

Spielberg is a Yang Fire Day Stem. The Yin Rival Sitting on the Birth Pillar Yin Fire Rooster is present in the Hour. Spielberg has three sisters: Sue, Anne and Nancy.

Example 8.9

Lindsay Lohan, American Actress and Singer,
July 2, 1986, 04:40 hours

Hour	Day	Month	Year
壬	丁	甲	丙
Yang Water	**Yin Fire**	Yang Wood	**Yang Fire**
寅	未	午	寅
Tiger	Sheep	Horse	**Tiger**

Lohan is a Yin Fire Day Stem. The Yang Rival Sitting on the Birth Pillar Yang Fire Tiger is present in the Year. Lohan has three younger siblings: sister Ali and brothers Michael Jr. and Cody.

Example 8.10

Harrison Ford, American Actor, July 13, 1942, 11:41 hours

Hour	Day	Month	Year
丙	丁	丁	壬
Yang Fire	**Yin Fire**	Yin Fire	Yang Water
午	卯	未	午
Horse	Rabbit	Sheep	Horse

Ford is a Yin Fire Day Stem. The Yang Rival Sitting on the Peak Pillar Yang Fire Horse is present in the Hour. Ford has a younger brother, Terence.

Example 8.11

Serena Williams, American Tennis Player, September 26, 1981, 20:28 hours

Hour	Day	Month	Year
庚	丁	丁	辛
Yang Metal	**Yin Fire**	**Yin Fire**	Yin Metal
戌	未	酉	酉
Dog	Sheep	**Rooster**	Rooster

Williams is a Yin Fire Day Stem. The Yin Rival Sitting on the Birth Pillar Yin Fire Rooster is present in the Month. Williams has older sister Venus, three maternal half sisters and two paternal half brothers.

Example 8.12

Steve Winwood, English Singer and Musician, May 12, 1948, 05:00 hours DST

Hour	Day	Month	Year
壬	丁	丁	戊
Yang Water	**Yin Fire**	**Yin Fire**	Yang Earth
寅	酉	巳	子
Tiger	Rooster	**Snake**	Rat

Winwood is a Yin Fire Day Stem. The Yin Rival Sitting on the Peak Yin Fire Snake is present in the Month. Winwood has an older brother, Muff.

Example 8.13

Dame Julie Walters, English Actress and Comedian, February 22, 1950, 15:00 hours

Hour	Day	Month	Year
庚	戊	戊	庚
Yang Metal	**Yang Earth**	**Yang Earth**	Yang Metal
申	子	寅	寅
Monkey	Rat	**Tiger**	Tiger

Walters is a Yang Earth Day Stem. The Yang Rival Sitting on the Birth Pillar Yang Earth Tiger is present in the Month. Walters has two older brothers, Tom and Kevin.

Example 8.14

Heidi Klum, German-American Model, June 1, 1973, 11:00 hours

Hour	Day	Month	Year
戊	戊	戊	癸
Yang Earth	**Yang Earth**	**Yang Earth**	Yin Water
午	辰	午	丑
Horse	Dragon	**Horse**	Ox

Klum is a Yang Earth Day Stem. The Yang Rival Sitting on the Peak Pillar Yang Earth Horse is present in the Month and Hour. Klum has an older brother, Michael.

Example 8.15

Lynn Anderson, American Country Singer,
September 26, 1947, 18:36 hours

Hour	Day	Month	Year
辛	**戊**	**己**	丁
Yin Metal	**Yang Earth**	**Yin Earth**	Yin Fire
酉	申	**酉**	亥
Rooster	Monkey	**Rooster**	Pig

Anderson is a Yang Earth Day Stem. The Yin Rival Sitting on the Birth Pillar Yin Earth Rooster is present in the Month. Anderson had an older sister, Liz.

Example 8.16

Fred Astaire, American Actor and Dancer,
May 10, 1899, 21:16 hours

Hour	Day	Month	Year
癸	**戊**	**己**	己
Yin Water	**Yang Earth**	**Yin Earth**	Yin Earth
亥	寅	**巳**	亥
Pig	Tiger	**Snake**	Pig

Astaire is a Yang Earth Day Stem. The Yin Rival Sitting on the Peak Pillar Yin Earth Snake is present in the Month. Astaire had an older sister, Adele.

Example 8.17

Drew Barrymore, American Actress and Filmmaker, February 22, 1975, 11:51 hours

Hour	Day	Month	Year
庚	己	戊	乙
Yang Metal	**Yin Earth**	**Yang Earth**	Yin Wood
午	亥	寅	卯
Horse	Pig	**Tiger**	Rabbit

Barrymore is a Yin Earth Day Stem. The Yang Rival Sitting on the Birth Pillar Yang Earth Tiger is present in the Month. Barrymore has three older paternal half siblings.

Example 8.18

Joyce Carol Oates, American Writer, June 16, 1938, 00:29 hours

Hour	Day	Month	Year
甲	己	戊	戊
Yang Wood	**Yin Earth**	**Yang Earth**	**Yang Earth**
子	卯	午	寅
Rat	Rabbit	**Horse**	**Tiger**

Oates is a Yin Earth Day Stem. The Yang Rival Sitting on the Birth Pillar Yang Earth Tiger is present in the Year. The Yang Rival Sitting on the Peak Pillar Yang Earth Horse is present in the Month. Oates has a younger brother, Fred Jr. and a younger sister, Lynn Ann.

Example 8.19

Heather Graham, American Actress,
January 29, 1970, 17:37 hours

Hour	Day	Month	Year
癸	己	丁	己
Yin Water	**Yin Earth**	Yin Fire	**Yin Earth**
酉	酉	丑	酉
Rooster	Rooster	Ox	**Rooster**

Graham is a Yin Earth Day Stem. The Yin Rival Sitting on the Birth Pillar Yin Earth Rooster is present in the Year. Graham has a younger sister, Aimee.

Example 8.20

Billy Joel, American Singer-Songwriter and Pianist,
May 9, 1949, 09:30 hours

Hour	Day	Month	Year
己	己	己	己
Yin Earth	**Yin Earth**	**Yin Earth**	Yin Earth
巳	亥	巳	丑
Snake	Pig	**Snake**	Ox

Joel is a Yin Earth Day Stem. The Yin Rival Sitting on the Peak Pillar Yin Earth Snake is present in the Month and Hour. Joel has a younger sister, Judith and a younger paternal half brother, Alexander.

Example 8.21

Jason Schwartzman, American Actor, June 26, 1980, 06:21 hours

Hour	Day	Month	Year
己	庚	壬	庚
Yin Earth	**Yang Metal**	Yang Water	**Yang Metal**
卯	午	午	申
Rabbit	Horse	Horse	**Monkey**

Schwartzman is a Yang Metal Day Stem. The Yang Rival Sitting on the Arrival Pillar Yang Metal Monkey is present in the Year. Schwartzman has a younger brother, Robert, paternal half-siblings Stephanie and John and maternal half brother Matthew Shire.

Example 8.22

Rami Malek, American Actor, May 12, 1981, 08:41 hours

Hour	Day	Month	Year
庚	庚	癸	辛
Yang Metal	**Yang Metal**	Yin Water	**Yin Metal**
辰	寅	巳	酉
Dragon	Tiger	Snake	**Rooster**

Malek is a Yang Metal Day Stem. The Yin Rival Sitting on the Arrival Pillar Yin Metal Rooster is present in the Year. Malek has an older sister, Nelly and a younger identical twin brother, Sami.

Example 8.23

Brody Jenner, American Television Personality,
August 21, 1983, 11:55 hours DST

Hour	Day	Month	Year
癸	辛	庚	癸
Yin Water	**Yin Metal**	**Yang Metal**	Yin Water
巳	巳	申	亥
Snake	Snake	**Monkey**	Pig

Jenner is a Yin Metal Day Stem. The Yang Rival Sitting on the Arrival Pillar Yang Metal Monkey is present in the Month. Jenner has an older brother Brandon, two older paternal half-siblings Burt and Cassandra and two younger paternal half sisters Kylie and Kendall.

Example 8.24

Naomi Watts, British Actress,
September 28, 1968, 11:00 hours DST

Hour	Day	Month	Year
癸	辛	辛	戊
Yin Water	**Yin Metal**	**Yin Metal**	Yang Earth
巳	丑	酉	申
Snake	Ox	**Rooster**	Monkey

Watts is a Yin Metal Day Stem. The Yin Rival Sitting on the Arrival Pillar Yin Metal Rooster is present in the Month. Watts has an older brother, Ben.

Example 8.25

Ellen Burstyn, American Actress,
December 7, 1932, 04:00 hours

Hour	Day	Month	Year
壬	壬	壬	壬
Yang Water	Yang Water	Yang Water	Yang Water
寅	寅	子	申
Tiger	Tiger	Rat	Monkey

Burstyn is a Yang Water Day Stem. The Yang Rival Sitting on the Birth Pillar Yang Water Monkey is present in the Year. The Yang Rival Sitting on the Peak Pillar Yang Water Rat is present in the Month. Burstyn has an older brother, Jack and a younger brother, Steve.

Example 8.26

Gerard Butler, Scottish Actor,
November 13, 1969, 05:21 hours

Hour	Day	Month	Year
癸	壬	乙	己
Yin Water	Yang Water	Yin Wood	Yin Earth
卯	辰	亥	酉
Rabbit	Dragon	Pig	Rooster

Butler is a Yang Water Day Stem. The Yin Rival Sitting on the Birth Pillar Yin Water Rabbit is present in the Hour. Butler is the youngest of three children, he has an older brother and sister.

Example 8.27

Miranda Lambert, American Country Singer,
November 10, 1983, 00:08 hours

Hour	Day	Month	Year
庚	壬	癸	癸
Yang Metal	**Yang Water**	**Yin Water**	**Yin Water**
子	寅	亥	亥
Rat	Tiger	**Pig**	**Pig**

Lambert is a Yang Water Day Stem. The Yin Rival Sitting on the Peak Pillar Yin Water Pig is present in the Year and Month. Lambert has a brother, Luke.

Example 8.28

Amy Adams, American Actress,
August 20, 1974, 00:00 hours

Hour	Day	Month	Year
壬	癸	壬	甲
Yang Water	Yin Water	**Yang Water**	Yang Wood
子	巳	申	寅
Rat	Snake	**Monkey**	Tiger

Adams is a Yin Water Day Stem. The Yang Rival Sitting on the Birth Pillar Yang Water Monkey is present in the Month. The Yang Rival Sitting on the Peak Pillar Yang Water Rat is present in the Hour. Adams has four brothers and two sisters.

Example 8.29

Billy Dee Williams, American Actor, April 6, 1937, 21:51 hours

Hour	Day	Month	Year
癸	癸	癸	丁
Yin Water	**Yin Water**	**Yin Water**	Yin Fire
亥	亥	卯	丑
Pig	Pig	**Rabbit**	Ox

Williams is a Yin Water Day Stem. The Yin Rival Sitting on the Birth Pillar Yin Water Rabbit is present in the Month. The Yin Rival Sitting on the Peak Pillar Yin Water Pig is present in the Hour. Williams has a twin sister, Loreta.

Example 8.30

Henry Cavill, British Actor, May 5, 1983, 02:40 hours

Hour	Day	Month	Year
癸	癸	丙	癸
Yin Water	**Yin Water**	Yang Fire	**Yin Water**
丑	巳	辰	亥
Ox	Snake	Dragon	**Pig**

Cavill is a Yin Water Day Stem. The Yin Rival Sitting on the Peak Pillar Yin Water Pig is present in the Year. Cavill is the fourth of five boys, his brothers are Niki, Charlie, Piers and Simon.

Summary

In summary, what to look for in a chart with regard to the Rivals:

1. Rivals Sitting on the Birth, Arrival or Peak Pillar.

玖

Chapter Nine

Chapter Nine Conclusion

In conclusion, the following checklist indicates what to look for in a chart with regard to the Ten Gods:

Direct Power

1. Direct Power Sitting on the Nobleman Star.
2. Direct Power as a Solar or Lunar Helper.
3. Direct Power Sitting on the Academic Star.
4. Direct Power Sitting on the Prosperity Pillar.
5. Days Sitting on the Wealth and Direct Power.

Seven Killings

1. Seven Killings Sitting on the Earth Branch in the Year Pillar indicates a person born into modest circumstances who was able to improve their social and economic status.
2. Seven Killings Sitting on the Earth Branch in the Hour Pillar indicates good fortune.
3. Seven Killings present in the Hour Pillar (Stem, Branch or both) indicates a good reputation.

Eating God

1. Eating God Sitting on the Earth Branch.
2. Eating God Combination Pillar.
3. Eating God Sitting on the Birth Branch.
4. Eating God in a Stem Combination.

Hurting Officer

1. Hurting Officer Sitting on Resource Pillar.
2. Days Sitting on the Hurting Officer.

Wealth

1. Wealth hidden in the Branches.
2. Yang Day Stem Combinations with Wealth.
3. Indirect Wealth in the Month or Hour Stem.

Resource

1. Resource Sitting on the Birth Pillar.
2. Resource Sitting on the Seven Killings Pillar.

Rivals

1. Rivals Sitting on the Birth, Arrival or Peak.

www.ingramcontent.com/pod-product-compliance
Lightning Source LLC
Chambersburg PA
CBHW020406230426
43664CB00009B/1207